JOHN LENN

LENNO
OPENING HIS HEART AND MIND ON EVERYTHING
YOU'VE ALWAYS WANTED TO KNOW.

* WHAT WAS REALLY BEHIND THE BEATLES' BREAKUP?

* DID HE FEEL THAT PAUL HAD BETRAYED HIM?

* THE BUSINESS SCANDAL THAT LOST THE BEATLES THE RIGHTS TO MANY OF THEIR GREATEST SONGS.

* THE CRAZY, UNBELIEVABLE EARLY DAYS IN LIVERPOOL AND HAMBURG—INCLUDING THE NIGHT HE PERFORMED IN HIS UNDER-WEAR.

* THE ROLE OF DRUGS IN THEIR MUSIC.

* HIS LIFE WITH YOKO.

* THE REAL STORY BEHIND THE LENNON–McCARTNEY SONGWRITING TEAM.

* WHY THERE WAS NEVER ANY CHANCE OF A BEATLES REUNION.

* AND MUCH, MUCH MORE!

JOHN LENNON:
FOR THE RECORD

Peter McCabe
and
Robert D. Schonfeld

Bantam Books
Toronto • New York • London • Sydney • Auckland

JOHN LENNON: FOR THE RECORD

A Bantam Book / September 1984
A portion of this book appeared in PENTHOUSE,
September 1984 issue

Cover artwork by Kunio Hagio.

ISBN 0-553-24802-2

Published simultaneously in the United States
and Canada

Bantam Books are published by Bantam Books, Inc.
Its trademark, consisting of the words "Bantam Books"
and the portrayal of a rooster, is Registered in
U.S. Patent and Trademark Office and in other
countries. Marca Registrada. Bantam Books, Inc.,
666 Fifth Avenue, New York, New York 10103.

PRINTED IN THE UNITED STATES OF AMERICA

H   0 9 8 7 6 5 4 3 2 1

For my son, Jason, my parents, and friends.
—P.M.

For Mrs. B.
—R.D.S.

INTRODUCTION

by Peter McCabe

John Lennon first met Yoko Ono at a London art gallery in 1967. At that time he was in the heyday of his recording career as a Beatle, and he was recognized the world over as one of the greatest writers ever of popular music. On the day he entered the gallery, he walked over to a ladder, climbed it, picked up a magnifying glass, and read some tiny lettering on a canvas. It read "Yes." He was then introduced to the artist, and so began a liaison the world would hear a lot about.

In those days the name Yoko Ono meant little outside the New York art world. Yoko was from a conservative Japanese family that had moved to New York when she was nineteen. She had gone to Sarah Lawrence, dropped out and married a Japanese musician, then divorced him to marry an American filmmaker, Tony Cox, by whom she had a daughter. Her work was avant-garde and it fascinated John. The rest of the Beatles would soon have to contend with the couple's togetherness, as John and Yoko went off in new directions with a series of exhibitionist events.

John and Yoko had been together four years when they gave us this interview. It took place over two sessions at the St. Regis Hotel in New York in the summer of 1971. My coauthor, Bob Schonfeld, and I spent nearly three months setting it up, and, ironically, when it was done we never published it. At the time we were writing a book about the series of business disputes, corporate takeovers, and "family squabbles" that led to the Beatles' breakup. By the time this interview was granted, the book was nearly written, and we used the material from it only as background. The interview itself remained, until now, on a closet shelf.

In the spring of 1971 we spent several months interviewing various members of the Beatle entourage as we researched our book. We met with Allen Klein, who by then was managing three Beatles, and we talked with Lee and John Eastman (Paul McCartney's father-in-law and brother-in-law), whom Paul wanted to handle the Beatles' business affairs. We talked with a lot of men who had battled with the Beatles and with each other for control of the very valuable Beatle song copyrights, "men in suits," as John had described them, "sitting on their fat arses in the city." We met briefly with George and Ringo, and with John and Yoko, at Allen

Klein's office, and we tried to talk to Paul, but Paul would only speak through his in-laws. John and Yoko agreed to talk with us at much greater length, but as often is the case with John and Yoko, it was a question of pinning them down.

In a sense, we later realized, we were being put to the test. They (Klein, John, and Yoko) wanted to see what information we could obtain on our own, by digging. And so we dug through legal briefs and takeover prospectuses, and we traveled back and forth between the Apple offices in London and New York, and we talked with ex-Beatle employees and advisers, and we had our own meetings with gray-suited bankers, including one in his Hampstead home who said he had hoped to "harness the Beatles" to make sure they would "give the public what it wants." We met with Neil Aspinall, the Beatles' long-standing retainer and friend, and managing director of Apple. We met with Derek Taylor, who had headed Beatle PR, and who recently had quit working for the Beatles. We spoke to dozens of people who had known the Beatles over the years, including Nat Weiss, who was Brian Epstein's partner; Sid Bernstein, who promoted the Beatles' first American concerts; and Al Brodax, who produced *Yellow Submarine.* We talked to Epstein's family, and to Lillian Roxon, the rock critic who was a close friend of Linda Eastman's, and to John Donbar, who introduced John to Yoko, and so on, and so forth. . . .

We digested all this information and opinion, and we put together our book. It was published in 1972, and was seen as insightful and slightly cruel. "Penetrating in its outlining of the Beatles' commercial woes," wrote *The New York Times* reviewer, who then went on to chastise us for dealing in backstairs gossip.

There was, of course, enormous public interest in the Beatles' much publicized breakup. After all, they were the greatest musical, perhaps cultural, phenomenon of the 1960s. Their appeal reached across generations, their influence on music, styles, and attitudes was huge, and they had brought rock, almost single-handedly, to its dominant position in popular entertainment. But by the time of our writing, the Beatles were in ruins—at least as a single entity. They were fighting among themselves, their business ventures had collapsed, their old brash confidence was gone: they just seemed sad.

After the years of touring, after successful album upon successful album, their purported enormous wealth was a mere fraction of what the public supposed it to be. They were still rich by any standard, but they had lost control of their song copyrights to Sir Lew Grade of ATV, after a long-drawn-out takeover battle.

Their much publicized Apple venture had turned into a hopeless drain on their capital, a nightmare from which John finally emerged screaming "Help!"—a cry that was heeded by Allen Klein. They were struggling to clean house at Apple and put their financial affairs in shape when they began fighting among themselves.

It wasn't a minor dispute either. Personality differences between John and Paul, the enforced group identification of all those years, were starting to tell, and Brian Epstein, their manager, wasn't around anymore to make sure the center held. Epstein had died in 1967 from an overdose of sleeping pills, and although John says in this interview that Brian was never strong enough to "overbear" the Beatles, he had always been able to marshal them together by virtue of who he was.

Had Epstein lived, it is conceivable that he might have been able to find a solution to the differences between John and Paul. He might have found a compromise by which the Beatles could have recorded individually and also continued to record together. But who knows? The White Album is testament to their growing need to write and record separately. In fact, as John says in this interview, he and Paul wrote separately far more than the public ever imagined. And although it was Paul who was the first to go off alone and record a solo album, John had been chomping at the bit to do the same for a long time. He says he felt his creative juices flowing as they hadn't flowed in some time, and he ascribes this to Yoko's arrival on the scene. Maybe he is being modest, because he wrote "Penny Lane" and "Strawberry Fields" during that period that he appears to think of as not particularly creative, but in any event he claims he was moving in new directions, and he credits Yoko with having provided him with the impetus.

One could hardly understate the size of the rift between John and Paul McCartney. It took on every aspect of a celebrity divorce, the kind that gets covered in detail in the pages of *People* or the *National Inquirer*. Paul went into court, seeking to dissolve the Beatles' partnership, and John, knowing Paul's close-to-the-bone negative publicity, reacted by hanging out all the dirty linen. Paul, typically, did his best to smooth his feathers and try to act as unruffled as possible.

During the course of one of our interviews we had a chance to listen (with the tape recorder off at the time) to one chapter of the dispute that was being conducted over the telephone. By this time, the matter of the dissolution of the Beatles' partnership was all but complete. What was still going on was the conflict between John and Paul, a personality conflict. Every blame was being apportioned, every difference pointed out. They were almost diametrically opposed, musically, philosophically, in all matters of taste and style. John was running around New York, mixing with the avant-garde and the radicals, taking up causes and politicizing his songs. Paul was safely in the arms of Linda and the Eastmans, dividing his time between his home in Scotland and Park Avenue, and recording songs that often fell neatly into a category of rock called bubble gum. McCartney's in-laws (lawyers both) had experience in music publishing, and Paul had seen no reason not to have them handling the Beatles' business. But to John, the Eastmans were anathema. He couldn't stand them, seeing them as the kind of people he had crossed swords with in the City of London, the people whose posture was "we're here to help you." He decided that the Eastmans were continually interfering with the deals that Klein was trying to negotiate on behalf of all the Beatles, and finally he lambasted them publicly in no uncertain terms, ending once and for all any possibility of a compromise. Klein, on the other hand, he was drawn to—Klein the orphan, Klein the underdog, Klein the man the establishment didn't trust.

When the case went to court, Paul won. The Beatles were legally torn apart. The dissolution was complete. John and Paul would never write or record together again. The Beatles would never appear again on the same stage. George moved to the forefront as a soloist, and Ringo took part in a few movies and had a hit single. Paul blended neatly into the rock scene, and continued to be a fixture on the charts. John, after eighteen months of separation from Yoko, returned to her, had a son, Sean, by her, then largely eschewed the rock world, turned his business affairs over to his wife, and devoted himself to his son. He recorded less. He appeared to be on the verge of coming out of his seclusion when he was shot to death outside his apartment building in New York, on December 8, 1980.

The day after John died, I was asked by a couple of magazines to write a piece about him. I wasn't up for it. I was also asked about these tapes, and at the time it didn't occur to me to publish them. One magazine happened to be running an interview with John when he was killed, and enough tributes were being paid without another one being added.

Even writing now, I think it best to leave the quality of John's chord progressions to the musicologists. What I offer instead is a number of impressions from short acquaintance. I met John, liked him, and got to know him a bit. I think he opened up for this interview in part because I grew up in Liverpool as he did.

My impressions go way back. My earliest memories go back to a band known at the time as the "Silver Beatles." With friends, I would take the ferry across the Mersey, catch a bus to Matthew Street, descend into the abandoned, bricked-off sewer that was the Cavern Club, and listen to that Beatle "sound," as John always called it, in the hundred-degree crush of bodies. I was fifteen. I wore tight jeans, a black imitation leather jacket, and pointed shoes called winklepickers. The jacket did little to protect me from the chill when I emerged into the Liverpool night. I had to take the ferry home, and my mother, finding my sweat-stained shirt, would yell: "You'll die of pneumonia going to that place!"

In late 1961, my family moved fifteen miles from Liverpool. I didn't see the Beatles for about a year. The next time I saw them, it was late 1962, when they played a big dance hall near where I lived. The Riverside Lounge—I remember it was a tough place. There were always fights there. I had a friend in high school, an Elvis fan, and I persuaded him to go with me. I had been reading in *Merseybeat*, the local rock newspaper, that the Beatles had acquired a huge following. Word hadn't reached the town I had moved to; the dance hall was half empty. The "sound," however, was no less wonderful, far and above that of any other local band, and that night the Beatles made a point of introducing their new drummer, who had been with them only a few dates. Paul was stage right, I remember, and being very communicative, in much the same way he is today in his MTV videos. John was more distant, tougher, a loud leather-lunged presence. They sang "Anna" and ended with "Twist and Shout." And when I got home I recall my father talking to us about the Cuban Missile Crisis, unaware that a chapter in history was taking place just down the road.

A few months later, I opened the *New Musical Express* to find that "Love Me Do" was number seventeen on the British charts. It didn't climb much higher, but the second single, "Please, Please Me," made it all the way to number one. That following summer, 1963, I fell in love to the strains of "She Loves You," and the country went into its throes of Beatlemania. For the next eight years my insights and perceptions of the Beatles would be the same as that of the world at large.

When we turned up at the St. Regis for our first interview, John and Yoko were still in bed. It was early afternoon, and there was a flurry of activity in the adjacent suite of rooms, as Beatle assistants made ready to show the couple a project that had been completed that morning. May Pang was much in evidence, bustling about the suite getting things ready, her long black hair swirling around her. (This was a year or two before her affair with John.) She told us that our interview would have to be interrupted by a fitting for Yoko, and it turned out this worked to our advantage. Together, John and Yoko tended to concentrate on recent events, but in Yoko's absence the interview took a different turn, as John (with a few nudgings) went back into the past with a long narrative about Hamburg, his early writings, and the role of Brian Epstein.

We were served tea on silver trays. John chain-smoked Gauloises, and he and Yoko remained in bed in their bathrobes. We were put through a few preliminaries before we turned the tape recorder on. John wanted to know what our research had turned up, and what Klein and the Eastmans, among others, had told us. He was hoping we could obtain an interview with Paul, suggesting among other things that we talk to Paul's brother, Mike McGear, with whom John obviously was still good friends. "Mike's an intelligent guy," he said. "And he could give you some insights into Paul's character." The McGear contact failed, however. Paul was talking only through the Eastmans.

And so the interview proceeded, the actual taped parts being conducted at the St. Regis. Other nontaped conversations took place at dinner, in Allen Klein's office, and at a recording session. John's intention throughout the interviews was to set the record straight. Occasionally he would disclose a piece of information that he did not want on the record, and the tape recorder would have to go off while he told an anecdote that shed light on a particular subject. But for the most part it was typical John: let the truth be told.

One topic he declined to go into in any detail was George Harrison's role. He was nervous generally about what he had said about George in this interview, and when I pushed him for a candid assessment of George, he said he had talked enough. At the time I felt there was tension between himself and George. It later turned out that they had indeed had some differences. George had delivered a number of unflattering remarks about John, and John resented this. He felt George was ungrateful. After all, hadn't he helped and encouraged George musically for many years?

Paul, on the other hand, he had no qualms about attacking. Why not? The dice were cast. But when I played the tapes later, I noticed he never had a bad thing to say about Paul's music. He attacked Paul for being bossy, arrogant, and chauvinistic, for failing to stand up to his father, for being a dupe of the Eastmans', but he never had anything negative to say about Paul's abilities as a songwriter or recording artist. And even with the attacks, he would be telling us in the next breath about Paul having to be on stage in Hamburg for an hour and a half playing "What'd I Say," and you could hear the affection in his voice.

This alternating cut-and-praise style of John's was directed at others as well. He said of Brian Epstein: "Brian definitely looked after himself and not us," but he also said: "Brian seemed a great manager, and in the group I was closest to him." Of Derek Taylor, he said: "We were his gravy train," then a half hour later he would be telling us a wonderful anecdote, and attributing its origin to Derek. He said about rock critic Lillian Roxon, who had written something negative about him, "I'll probably outlast her," then he went on to add that Lillian's book, *Rock Encyclopedia,* was probably the best book on the subject of rock and roll."

I have listened to these tapes many times, know every inflection by heart almost, and I am struck at times by the contradictions within John Lennon. He tended to see the world in terms of black and white, and people were either on his good list or his hit list, often subject to being switched at a moment's notice, according to which way the conversation turned. What came across during our interviews was that he was a lot more defensive than I had imagined, and being intelligent and glib, he marshaled his barbs quickly when he felt he was being attacked.

He was always outspoken, whether he was being critical or complimentary, and I am sure he will be remembered for his candor, as well as his music. Yet the charm of John's outspokenness was not only his way with words, but the fact that he was as critical and candid about himself as about others. In the end it was this that made him endearing. He bared his soul about everything, about his insecurities, his temper, his mistakes, and when he did so, even when he appeared ridiculous, he breathed fresh air into the entertainment world.

He could be vain and egotistical, and there are many stories about John that make a mockery of his being "one of the people." Once when we were having dinner, he got so caught up in his monologue, talking full steam, that he thought nothing of asking the waiter to cut his steak into "bite-size pieces." Yet he was often remarkably modest about the thing he was most renowned for: his music. In this interview, for example, when he was talking of how Allen Klein gained access to him and took over as manager, he said: "He [Klein] knew all my lyrics, and he understood them." Then he added: "not that there's much to understand." As I listened to him talking for this interview and on other occasions, it dawned on me that he really did not think to compare himself to Gershwin or Porter, or to any of the greats of twentieth-century popular music, of which undoubtedly he is one. I am not saying he wasn't proud of his work, because in other interviews he has said he was, but I found that he could easily dismiss compositions, which the world still hums two decades later, with the words, "It was never very good in the first place."

Is this naïveté? I suspect it was. Throughout his life John retained boyish qualities. His naïveté was very visible when he first came to New York to live, and he proceeded to entertain a parade of con artists, Jerry Rubin and the like, who got close to him for a while. But he knew he could be easily conned. He says so in this interview.

He also says he admired the "con artist" in Yoko, insofar as she exhibited this in her work. Yoko did not contest this. On the contrary. Yes, she said, I am a con artist. That's what a lot of my work is about. I'm not a concept artist, I'm a con artist.

At this point in the discussion both John and Yoko were leaning toward the microphone, each jostling the other to tell their side of the story of how they met and fell in love. Each was talking about the effect they had had on the other. I doubt that anybody could have been in their presence for those few minutes and ever be able to think subsequently that Yoko "conned" John into loving her, or that she didn't love him. Granted their "togetherness" was tiresome at times, but it never seems to have occurred to the Yoko detractors, nor to the legions of Beatle fans who still wanted to see John "married" to Paul, that John Lennon, who was never easily satisfied, was not the sort of person to stick with someone he didn't ultimately deem good for himself. Whatever people may dislike about Yoko, at least give her points for that.

Yoko can be maddeningly persistent. Sometimes her way of explaining herself is off-putting. She goes on and on and on when she wants to make a point. She is a practitioner of the stunt, and people see her as transparent. The truth is: successful promotion comes in more subtle guises than Yoko Ono.

She is an egotist, and a feminist, and one can readily see why her art has only limited appeal, no matter how hard she hustles. There are some who say that her influence had a negative effect on John's music, but this seems absurd to me. John's songs "Imagine" and "All Across the Universe," and several other songs he wrote while with Yoko, are as good as any songs he wrote as a Beatle.

Yoko is extremely intelligent, and possessed of considerable insight. For the record, I found her often to be wry, charming, and subtle. She is also capable of being forthright in the extreme, but in this respect she was every bit a match for John. She makes no effort to conceal her desire to be successful, and according to those who knew her before she met John, she never did. If this is a character flaw, or a failure of PR, so be it.

I tend to think that after she met John, she brought him beyond the adolescent and all-too-chauvinistic world of rock and roll. John paid many prices for being a Beatle. As Neil Aspinall said, "The Beatles' world was an unreal world, a war zone." In a way, I think Yoko brought John home. He found comfort, love, and understanding with her, and he had a son by her, and he devoted himself to the child. He had not been able to do this with his other son, Julian, by Cynthia, and I think he was a much happier man in 1980 than he was in 1967 when he walked into that London gallery to see Yoko's art show.

John says in this interview: "It had to take that special combination of Paul, John, George, and Ringo to make the Beatles. There's no such thing as 'Well, John and Paul wrote all the songs, so therefore they contributed more.'" This may be true, but as this interview makes plain, without John's energy there may never have been a Beatles. McCartney at one time thought seriously about taking a steady job. John was always the one to take risks, he was generally the most aware, and so many of the Beatles' stylistic influences, musical and otherwise, were drawn from him. John Lennon's voice was heard in song, in jest, in protest, questioning every aspect of the culture he was at the same time influencing. He was widely heeded, and eminently quotable, and he lived life as it should be: to the fullest.

Malcolm Muggeridge was once asked to list the important things he had learned at age seventy-five. He began by saying, "Life should be a drama, not a process." John Lennon's life was eloquent testament to that statement, and as the most unlikely figure of Sir Lew Grade said: "Those songs in Northern [Songs] will live on forever." And as the man who now profits from them, he should know.

As John said: "A working-class hero is something to be."

FOREWORD

by Robert D. Schonfeld

Before I met John Lennon, my favorite Beatle fantasy was that they would hold a reunion concert in New York. The lights would go down, the crowd would catch its breath, then the lights would come on, and they would open up with "Sergeant Pepper," Paul giving the downbeat in that clipped, pure-rock cadence. Then the rasping, grinding guitar line, and then: "It was twenty years ago today . . ."

Knowing I was going to interview John, I even had hopes of talking him into my fantasy. Then I met him, and I realized it was not to be. At the time I was an MBA candidate at New York University. I was in training to become one of the "men in suits" he so despised at the time of this interview. My friends included a number of business-people-to-be, and some of them were laid out bleeding in an antiwar protest around the Stock Exchange. But I don't think this would have mitigated one bit John's bitterness about business people and the way his affairs had been managed, or more aptly, mismanaged. Trust had been misplaced. Confidence had been lost. Where did one decide to place one's faith?

The question, easily asked, held little hope for an answer. Of course it was all a matter of people-picking, but there are no schools in people-picking. In the late sixties and early seventies, the chameleon was very much abroad in the land. Plenty of the "men in suits" didn't wear suits; some didn't even wear shoes. For John, this confusion became an obstacle to creativity. For a while it resulted in disillusionment.

It was only later, when I began my career as an art dealer, that I realized that the primary responsibility of those who provide support systems to artists is to contribute to an environment that allows the artist maximum freedom of expression. Who provided this for John? Ultimately, it was Yoko. "The dragon lady who broke up the Beatles" turned out to be the one providing the best support system of all. In this sense she was his best manager. She satisfied his needs and saw to his affairs, and left him freer to give of himself, which he did. All of us are the richer for it.

Int.: So the dream is over, the Beatles have split up and you're now a separate entity from Paul McCartney. How does it feel?

John: Well, it's not over yet. With the court case, it could go on for years. And I guess every time I put a record out they'll compare it to Paul's.

Int.: Does that bother you?

John: Sure. What's the fucking point? You might as well compare me with Grand Funk Railroad or something.

Int.: You've been especially vocal lately about the way the Beatles' business was run in the past.

John: Well, look what happened. With Northern Songs, we ended up selling half our copyrights forever. We lost 'em all and Lew Grade's got 'em. It was bad management. We have no company. That's where Brian

Epstein fucked up. Who got the benefit? Not us. I mean, since you ask, in retrospect he made mistakes. But to us he was the expert. I mean, originally he had a shop. Anybody who's got a shop must be all right.

Int.: People say it was Epstein who kept you together as the Beatles. What was the mood like among you all after the Beatles stopped touring and before Brian died?

John: Well, after we stopped touring, it always seemed embarrassing. Should we have dinner together? It always got so formal that none of us wanted to go through with it anymore.

Int.: How come it got so formal?

John: Because when you don't see someone for a few months, you feel stilted and you have to start again.

Int.: So things were breaking down before you met Yoko, and before Paul met Linda?

John: It had broken down before that. There was a Liverpool clique thing, and everybody who worked for us was from Liverpool. But that togetherness had gone a long time before Yoko. We were really all on our own, just living in separate vacuums.

Int.: So let's talk about the Beatles' breakup, and the falling out between you and Paul. A lot of people think it had to do with the women in your lives. Is that why the Beatles split up?

John: Not really. The split was over who would manage us, Allen Klein or the Eastmans, and nothing else really, although the split had been coming from *Pepper* onwards.

Int.: Why, specifically?

John: Well, Paul was always upset about the White Album. He never liked it because on that one I did my music, he did his, and George did his. And first, he didn't like George having so many tracks, and second, he wanted it to be more a group thing, which really means more Paul. So he never liked that album, and I always preferred it to all the other albums, including *Pepper*, because I thought the music was better. The *Pepper* myth is bigger, but the music on the *White Album* is far superior, I think.

Int.: That's your favorite, of all the Beatle albums?

John: Yeah, because I wrote a lot of good shit on that. I like all the stuff I did on that, and the other stuff as well. I like the whole album. I haven't heard it in a long time, but I know there's a lot of good songs on it. But if you're talking about the split, the split was over Allen and Eastman.

Int.: You didn't like Lee Eastman, Linda's father, nor John Eastman, Linda's brother, and the Eastmans didn't like you bringing in Allen Klein to manage you. . . .

John: The Eastmans hated Allen from way back. They're from the class of family . . . like all classes, I suppose, they vote like Daddy does. They're the kind of kids who just think what their fathers told them.

Int.: But for a while you got along with Linda.

John: We all got along well with Linda.

Int.: When did you first meet her?

John: The first time I saw her was after that press conference to announce Apple in America. We were just going back to the airport and she was in the car with us. I didn't think she was particularly attractive, I wondered what he was bothering having her in the car for. A bit too tweedy, you know. But she sat in the car and took photographs and that was it. And the next minute she's married him.

Yoko: She's not the kind of woman who would antagonize other women. She is a nice person who is uptight like her brother, John, but not that uptight. There was a nice quality about her. As a woman she doesn't offend you because she doesn't come on like a coquettish bird, you know? So she was all right, and we were on very good terms until Allen came into the picture. And then she said: "Why the hell do you have to bring Allen into it?" She said very nasty things about Allen, and I defended Allen each time she said something about him. And since then she never speaks to me.

Int.: Yoko, you weren't with John the first time he met her?

Yoko: No. The first time I met her was when she came to the EMI studio. And you know, when Beatles are recording, there's very few people around, especially no women. If a young woman comes into the room, everybody just sort of looks at her. So I was there, and the first thing Linda made clear to me—almost unnecessarily—was the fact that she was interested in Paul, and not John, you know? So I thought that was nice. She was sort of presupposing that I would be nervous. Not that I showed

I was nervous at all. She just said, "Oh, I'm with Paul." Something to that effect.

I think she was eager to be with me, and John, in the sense that Paul and John are close, we should be close too. And couple to couple we were going to be good friends. We went to their house. . . .

John: We stayed there. We lived there.

Yoko: Well, that was not when Linda was around.

John: Oh, that was before Linda, yes.

Yoko: And Linda cooked for us. We had nice dinners together, things like that. And she was pregnant, so it was hard for her to cook. She had a big tummy and all that. But she was doing it, and it was nice.

Int.: Did you think she was a good photographer, Yoko?

Yoko: I never judged her, or even observed her, from that point of view. I'd never really seen any of her photographs.

John: We had heard stories about her hanging around—what was it?—*Ramparts* and *Life* magazine. Always trying to get in, and nobody wanting her because they didn't think she was a particularly good photographer. . . .

Yoko: They were sufficient photographs. And really, it's unfair to ask me about them because I'm a perfectionist about artists, and there are very few artists that I respect anyway. It has to be someone really special for me to say that I admire his or her art.

Int.: So what was Paul's attitude to you as you got to know him, as things progressed?

Yoko: Paul began complaining that I was sitting too close to them when they were recording, and that I should be in the background.

John: Paul was always gently coming up to Yoko and saying: "Why don't you keep in the background a bit more?" I didn't know what was going on. It was going on behind my back.

Yoko: And I wasn't uttering a word. It wasn't a matter of my being aggressive. It was just the fact that I was sitting near to John. And we stood up to it. We just said, "No. It's simply that we just have to come together." They were trying to discourage me from attending meetings, et cetera. And I was always there. And Linda actually said that she admired that we were doing that.

John: Paul even said that to me.

Int.: So did all this contribute to the split, to Paul leaving the group?

John: Well, Paul rang me up. He didn't actually tell me he'd split, he said he was putting out an album [*McCartney*]. He said, "I'm now doing what you and Yoko were doing last year. I understand what you were doing." All that shit. So I said, "Good luck to yer."

Yoko: So there really was a lot of misunderstanding, you know.

Int.: And the family thing was a factor? Things you'd said about the Eastmans?

John: Yeah, it's like anybody. If there's anything to say about my family, I'll say it myself. But don't you.

Int.: And Linda didn't like this?

Yoko: I didn't know that. I thought she was one very unusually obedient daughter who was completely controlled by her father, you know?

Int.: Was it the suddenness of Linda's arrival on the scene that disrupted things?

John: Well, Paul had met her before [the Apple press conference], you see. I mean, there were quite a few women he'd obviously had that I never knew about. God knows when he was doing it, but he must have been doing it.

Int.: So, John. You and Paul were probably the greatest songwriting team in a generation. And you had this huge falling out. Were there always huge differences between you and Paul, or was there a time when you had a lot in common?

John: Well, we all want our mummies—I don't think there's any of us that don't—and he lost his mother, so did I. That doesn't make womanizers of us, but we all want our mummies because I don't think any of us got enough of them.

Anyway, that's neither here nor there—but Paul always wanted the home life, you see. He liked it with daddy and the brother . . . and obviously missed his mother. And his dad was the whole thing. Just simple things: he wouldn't go against his dad and wear drainpipe trousers. And his dad was always trying to get me out of the group behind me back, I found out later. He'd say to George: "Why don't you get rid of John, he's just a lot of trouble. Cut your hair nice and wear baggy trousers," like I was the bad influence because I was the eldest, so I had all the gear first usually.

So Paul was always like that. And I was always saying, "Face up to your dad, tell him to fuck off. He can't hit you. You can kill him [laughs], he's an old man." I used to say, "Don't take that shit off him." Because I was always brought up by a woman, so maybe it was different. But I wouldn't let the old man treat me like that. He treated Paul like a child all the time, cut his hair and telling him what to wear, at seventeen, eighteen.

But Paul would always give in to his dad. His dad told him to get a job, he fucking dropped the group and started working on the fucking lorries, saying, "I need a steady career." We couldn't believe it. So I said to him—my Aunt Mimi reminded me of this the other night—he rang up and said he'd got this job and couldn't come to the group. So I told him on the phone, "Either come or you're out." So he had to make a decision between me and his dad then, and in the end he chose me. But it was a long trip.

So it was always the family thing, you see. If Jane [Asher] was to have a career, then that's not going to be a cozy family, is it? All the other girls were just groupies mainly. And with Linda not only did he have a ready-made family, but she knows what he wants, obviously, and has given it to him. The complete family life. He's in Scotland. He told me he doesn't like English cities anymore. So that's how it is.

Int.: So you think with Linda he's found what he wanted?

John: I guess so. I guess so. I just don't understand . . . I never knew what he wanted in a woman because I never knew what I wanted. I knew I wanted something intelligent or something arty, whatever it was. But you don't really know what you want until you find it. So anyway, I was very surprised with Linda. I wouldn't have been surprised if he'd married Jane Asher, because it had been going on for a long time and they went through a whole ordinary love scene. But with Linda it was just like, boom! She was in and that was the end of it.

Int.: Did Paul put Jane off for many years, when she wanted to get married?

John: I have no idea. We never discussed our private lives like that. I never asked him. We'd got over "did you get a bit of tit?" and "what's happening?" All that scene. We didn't talk about it.

Int.: So Paul split, and your falling out was essentially with him?

John: Right.

Int.: So what made you decide not to participate in the Bangladesh concert with George and Ringo at Madison Square Garden? I mean, you were rather conspicuously absent.

John: Well, Allen [Klein] was putting it around that I ran off to England, so I wouldn't be there for the concert. But I told George about a week before it that I wouldn't be doing it. I just didn't feel like it. I just didn't want to be rehearsing and doing a big show-biz trip. We were in the Virgin Islands, and I certainly wasn't going to be rehearsing in New York, then going back to the Virgin Islands, then coming back up to New York and singing. And anyway, they couldn't have got any more people in, if I'd been there or not. I get enough money off records and I don't feel like doing two shows a night.

Int.: So what did you think of the concert?

John: I didn't see it. I mean, I haven't seen the movie. It seemed like a great success, you know. Newspaperwise it turned out great, and it seems like they got a lot of money. So it seemed all right, and from the reports of people there it seemed fine too. I didn't think much more about it really.

Int.: So when you say you don't feel like doing two shows a night, does this mean we've seen the end of live performances from John Lennon?

John: Oh, no. I want to do a big show. I feel like going out with Yoko. It's possible that a museum show of Yoko's, which is going on in Syracuse this October, will tour America, and it's possible that we'd be in the same town. The museum show is a really far-out scene, so if we do that, and if we are playing in the same place, we really could blow the town out.

See, George came up with a good idea after the concert, which I heard from Allen—I haven't talked to George about it—which was to take a big tour out, and do one show for free and one show for money, in each city. I thought that was good. Then I thought; "Well, fuck it. I don't want to earn any more money. I get enough off records. I don't want to do a big Apple/Beatle tour," because the thing I didn't like about the Bangladesh concert was that it was "the Beatles playing," and whatever it was they played, it wasn't the Beatles. So then I thought, "I'll go out on me own and take me own people with me."

Int.: So who would you take on tour with you ideally?"

John: Well, I'd like to go on the road with Jim Keltner, Klaus Voormann, Yoko, and Eric Clapton, if I can get him out of his house. And maybe when we've got it together, we'd decide if we'd want any saxophones or any kind of jazz like that. Or we might just play village squares or a nightclub.

Int.: Do you have any regrets about not doing the Bangladesh concert?

John: Well, in a way I regretted it. It would have been great, you know. And at first I thought: "Oh, I wish I'd been there. You know, with Dylan and Leon [Russell]. . . . they needed a rocker, and everybody was telling me, "You should have been there, John." I mean, Leon's a good rocker, but people were telling me, "You should have been there to weigh it up." But I'm glad I didn't do it in a way, because I didn't want to go on as the Beatles. And with George and Ringo there it would have been that connotation of Beatles—now let's hear Ringo sing "It Don't Come Easy." And that's why I left it all, so I wouldn't have to do all that. I don't want to play "My Sweet Lord." I'd as soon go out and do exactly what I want.

Yoko: Because we want to give them reality, you know. Not . . . "Oh, God."

John: And that is a conflict with George.

Int.: Since you mentioned that you'd go out on the road with Jim Keltner, a drummer, is that any reflection on Ringo's drumming?

John: Oh, no. I love his drumming. I think Keltner is technically a bit better, but Ringo is still one of the best drummers in rock.

Int.: John, you've said a couple of times already that you "get enough off records," yet not too long ago you were saying that you weren't anything like as rich as people thought you were. Are you rich enough finally?

John: Well, I do have money for the first time ever, really. I do feel slightly secure about it, secure enough to say I'll go on the road for free. The reason I got rich is because I'm so insecure. I couldn't give it all away, even in my most holy, Christian, God-fearing, Hare Krishna period. I got into that struggle: I should give it all away, I don't need it. But I need it because I'm so insecure. Yoko doesn't need it. She always had it. I have to have it. I'm not secure enough to give it all up, because I need it to protect me from whatever I'm frightened of.

Yoko: He's very vulnerable.

John: But now I think that Allen Klein has made me secure enough, it's his fault that I'll go out for free.

Int.: You mean tour for free?

John: Well, I thought I can't really go on the road and take a lot of money. (A) What am I going to do with it? And (B) how could I look somebody in the eye? Why should they pay? I've got everything I need. I've got all the fucking bread I need. If I go broke, well, I'd go on the road for money then. But now I just couldn't face saying, "Well, I cost a million when I sing. It costs that much for me to sing for you."

Yoko: It's criminal.

John: Which is bullshit, because I want to sing. So I'm going out on the road because I want to this time. I want to do something political, and radicalize people, and all that jazz, and this would be the best way. So now I feel like going out on the road. I feel like going out with Yoko, and taking a really far-out show on the road, a mobile, political, rock and roll show, a mobile, political Plastic Ono Bandshow. . . .

Yoko: With clowns as well.

John: . . . and have something going on in the foyer, and something going on in the audience, and not just everything on stage.

Int.: When you say political, what do you mean exactly?

John: Well, I mean political, because everything I do is political. I would take people with me who could speak to the kids, who could speak to them in the foyer, catch them on the way out. Panthers. Weathermen. They can hand all their gear out.

Int.: You want to create a riot in each town?

John: No, I don't want to create a riot or a fight in each town, but I just really want to paint it red.

Int.: So would these be big dates?

John: I don't know. I really haven't thought how to do it. You know what I was thinking—I know I've told you this before—when Paul's going out on the road, I'd like to be playing in the same town for free next door! And he's charging about a million to see him. That would be funny. And of course he's going to think that I'm going out on the road because he's said he's going out on the road, but it'd be a natural thing after Bangladesh.

Yoko: The point is, I really believe that whatever you have, if you don't do as much as you can or have, then you're guilty of not giving. Like, our position is, I come from the East, he comes from the West, a meeting of East and West, and all that. And to communicate with people is almost a responsibility. We actually are living proof of East and West getting along together. It's very important. We are responsible to give whatever we have, or whatever we know.

John: That's why I thought, I can't really go on the road and take a lot of money.

Yoko: No, we can't do that. If you have a lot to give, you have to give. Also, think of the laws of nature. In economic and political and all situations, high water falls low, you know. And if our cup is full, it's going to flow. It's natural for us to give because we have a lot. If we don't give, in a sense that's going against the laws of nature. And in order to go against the laws of nature, you have to use tremendous energy, unnecessary energy, in order to keep it like that, in order to keep that money. That would be very bad for us, and we're not going to do that. If we have more than we need moneywise, we'd rather let the money flow out naturally, you know.

Int.: That's a pretty generous sentiment.

Yoko: It's just wisdom, you know.

John: The wisdom of the East.

Yoko: And if people don't have that wisdom—well, what I mean is—if you're using all that unnecessary energy, it's going to get back at you one way or another. You're going to get cancer or something. And it just isn't worth it.

Int.: From what we've been reading, you are still asked regularly for a lot of money from various underground and leftist causes. Do you always give?

John: Well, I always take care of the underground, whatever I'm doing. And if they get in trouble, I lend them money or invest in them or whatever, because I think they're important. I get asked every two days for at least five thousand pounds, and I usually give it because it's usually somebody that I want to help. So I'm going to try to set up a foundation that can be small, a John and Yoko one, and we might take a dollar a head or anything that's donated at concerts. That would go to this. And then I can pay all these Oz undergrounds, and Clydeside workers, and Timothy Learys, that all want money out of me. And I might be able to fix it up taxwise.

George wants to do a foundation, too, but we'll keep it separate because he might want to give it to Hare Krishna, and I won't.

Int.: So you're going to tour for free, and you're going to give a lot of money away. How is your manager, Allen Klein, reacting to all this generosity?

John: I said to Allen, "You're going to get twenty percent of nothing." And I want him to run the tours because he knows how to do it. I said, "Look, I hope you won't mind, but you know George's idea about the concerts? Well, I've decided to do it all for nothing. And I'm sorry, but you're getting twenty percent of nothing." He said, "Oh, I don't mind." I don't know whether he did or not. Maybe he thinks he'll sell some comics on the side. He'll have thought of something.

Int.: Let's talk about Allen Klein because, as you said, the big factor in the Beatles' breakup was the question of who would manage you, Klein or the Eastmans. You, George, and Paul wanted Klein, and Paul wanted his in-laws. What made you opt for Klein?

John: Well, Allen's human, whereas Eastman and all them other people are automatons. Sure you can hurt Eastman's feelings, or anybody's feelings, but you can tickle Allen, and I can't imagine tickling Eastman.

Yoko: No sense of humor, Eastman's lot.

John: And when Allen's not doing his bit, he's one of the lads, you know. I would go on holiday with Allen, because he's a lad, he pisses about. When him and his crew go on tour, they piss about like school kids, pretending to be deaf and dumb, whatever kind of crazy thing. He's always having fun, trying to go into hotels with the wrong clothes, wearing crazy clothes. Just games like that. So he's good fun to be around, you know.

Yoko: Actually, he's shy and quiet.

John: And so insecure. He was an orphan. How insecure can you get, with nothing to hang on to?

Yoko: Can you imagine? He has to be a genius to make money. He was a penniless orphan.

John: And it's so easy to hurt him. It's just like Andy Warhol. Andy Warhol is a very sensitive guy, and if your tone of voice isn't right on the phone, he can get very upset and hurt, and think you're attacking him.

Well, Allen's just as bad as Andy Warhol. If you don't say it right, he gets very upset, he thinks you don't like him anymore. And I say, "That was a joke. I didn't mean that."

Yoko: But aside from that, he's a shy guy, very quiet inside. He talks a lot, but inside he's very quiet.

John: And like I say, he likes having a laugh with the lads, that sort of thing, whereas you can't imagine them others doing anything but playing golf or crushing beetles.

And one of the early things that impressed me about Allen—and obviously it was a kind of flattery as well—he went through all the old songs we'd written, and he really knew which stuff I'd written. Not many people knew which was my song and which was Paul's, but he'd say, "Well, McCartney didn't write that line, did he?" And I'd say, "Right," you know, and that's what really got me interested [in him], because he knew what our contributions were to the group. Most people thought it was all Paul, or all George Martin. And he knew all my lyrics, and he understood them, not that there's much to understand, but he was into it, and he dug lyrics. So I thought, "Well, anybody who knows me this well, just by listening to records, is pretty perceptive."

Yoko: Very perceptive.

John: Because I'm not the easiest guy to read, although I'm fairly naïve and open in some ways, and I can be conned easily. But in other ways I'm quite complicated, and it's not easy to get through all the defenses and see what I'm like. Klein knew me quite well, without even meeting me. Also he knew to come to me and not to go to Paul, whereas somebody like Lew Grade or Eastman would have gone to Paul.

So he knew that to get in he'd have to come through me. Mind you, he'd been sounding out Mick Jagger and Keith, and all them, saying, "Who runs what?"

Int.: So it's been a few years now since Allen Klein took over managing you and George and Ringo. What's your opinion of him as a manager?

John: Well, I love him, you know. I mean, he really has made me secure enough. I do have money for the first time ever, really. Sometimes he makes me very angry, like when he's pissed off, or pretends he's busy. At any rate, apart from that, I like him, you know. He's a great guy, highly sensitive, highly intelligent. He's not avant-garde or anything like that, he doesn't know from Adam. And it irritates me sometimes when I try and sing him a song before recording, and he can't hear it until it's a finished record. Or if I show him some rushes from a film, and he can't see it until it's a finished film. But apart from that I like him. I don't think he's robbing me, you know. I think he deserves twenty percent because that's his price.

Yoko: He's very creative.

John: He's a creative artist in the way that he will put people together, like Phil Spector and me, which was initially his doing. He tried to create a Rolling Stones/Beatles empire, which might have been a good thing in the early days.

Yoko: Not now.

John: Yeah, but it might have been a good thing. And that's the kind of thing he likes doing, you know. I believe him when he says he looks after Sam Cooke's old father. [Klein managed Sam Cooke, who was shot to death in a motel room.] I think he's a sentimental Jewish mommy, you know. He's got his bad points. He'll be there, and then he's gone, things like that. But he's got a lot of responsibility, and a lot of shit in his head. And it's people like him, or even Brian Epstein, who wasn't quite as clever as Allen, who can't delegate in a way. I know because even if I have a very intelligent assistant, if I piss off, it never gets done.

Int.: Let's talk a bit about Paul's aversion to Klein. From what we've read it seemed as if this wasn't there in the beginning, even though Paul wanted the Eastmans to run things. But it came on later as things progressed. And yet despite this, we gather that Klein was still hoping that Paul would return to the group.

John: Oh, he'd love it if Paul would come back. I think he was hoping he would for years and years. He thought that if he did something, to show Paul that he could do it, Paul would come around. But no chance.

I mean, *I* want him to come out of it, too, you know. He will one day. I give him five years, I've said that. In five years he'll wake up.

Int.: And yet Paul did pretty well from a number of deals Klein negotiated before Paul filed suit to dissolve the group partnership. And not the least of these was the renewed recording contract with EMI, which gave you all much higher royalties. What else was Klein doing to try and lure Paul back?

John: [laughs] One of his reasons for trying to get Paul back was that Paul would have forfeited his right to split by joining us again. We tried to con him into recording with us too. Allen came up with this plan. He said, "Just ring Paul and say, 'We're recording next Friday, are you coming?'" So it nearly happened. It got around that the Beatles were getting together again, because EMI heard that the Beatles had booked recording time again. But Paul would never, never do it, for anything, and now I would never do it. I'm not going to go on a concert tour with Paul, George, and Ringo, because I'm not going to resurrect that.

Int.: But Klein is still hoping?

John: He said to me, "Would you do it, if we got your immigration thing fixed? Or if we could get rid of the drug conviction?"

Yoko: And people don't understand, you know. There're so many groups that constantly announce they're going to split, they're going to split, and they can announce it every year, and it doesn't mean they're going to split. But people don't understand what an extraordinary position the Beatles are in, you know. In every way. They're in such an extraordinary position that they're more insecure than other people. And so Klein thinks he'll give Paul two years Lindawise, you know. And John said, "No, Paul treasures things like children, things like that. It will be longer." And of course, John was right.

Int.: We've heard that Klein has said that Linda and you, Yoko, were a large reason for the Beatles' breakup?

Yoko: Yeah, and I don't like it when Allen insinuates that Linda and me, being women, didn't get along, and that this was the cause of the split. It just isn't true.

John: Allen tries hard to understand Yoko and her work, but it's a struggle for him. He doesn't understand it. And it's taken him a long time to come around and realize she just isn't another chick, you know.

Yoko: Can you imagine that? John had a fever once and was asleep upstairs, and Allen visited us and was talking to me. And he said, "Well, you know, if I get to manage John and all that, if it works out that way, then I don't mind if John has a little fun on the side with you." He took me as a groupie chick, you know.

John: Because all the women he'd ever met with the groups were chicks.

Yoko: And I'm a Japanese girl, you know. That bit. So I thought, "What the hell. He didn't discover me yet."

John: He realizes she's intelligent. I think he knows you're proud. Now he's realizing she's not a chick. And if anything, at least his equal.

Yoko: I was laughing. I wasn't insulted. I thought, "My God, I must look young." I was almost flattered.

Int.: Still, in regard to Klein, there had been a tremendous outpouring of negative publicity about him, especially in the English press. And this went on for some time, as he was going after the Beatles. Didn't that bother you, or at least give you cause for reservation?

John: Well, he's a businessman. I feel sorry for him in the way I have some sympathy for Yoko, because it's difficult with all the attacks in the press. And the English do hate Americans and Jews, especially ones who are going to come in and make money in their little Wall Street, you know. They already beat Allen out once when he was trying to buy a music-publishing company. They clubbed together and got rid of him. So okay, he's probably cut many peoples' throats. So have I. I made it too. I mean, I can't remember anybody I literally cut, but I've certainly trod on a few feet on the way up. And I'm sure he did. I don't think he deserves the shit he gets thrown at him, and if time proves me wrong in the end, so be it. I think he deserves what he earns, and I do have more money.

Int.: You were making comparisons earlier between Klein and Brian Epstein. I want to talk more about Epstein later, but could we go on with the comparison?

Yoko: Well, Klein has this reputation as a whacky businessman, but I tell you, he's too conservative in many ways. That may surprise people but it's true. Klein's attitude is, he goes for the top people, right? He doesn't go for anybody but the top ... Rolling Stones, Beatles, et cetera. Which is all very good, but at the same time that means he doesn't take any risks.

John: He wouldn't have recognized us at the Cavern. And like the film *El Topo* ... we talked him into buying it, but he took our word that it was a good film.

Yoko: He would have been the guy who turned down the Beatles. . . .

John: No, he wouldn't. He can spot a good song when he hears it.

Int.: Aren't you really saying that he can only see the dollar signs?

Yoko: Right.

John: That's what it is.

Int.: Let's go back to that comparison with Epstein. You mentioned something about delegating.

John: Yeah. Well, Brian couldn't delegate, and neither can Allen. But what I was saying was, I understand that because when I try and delegate it never gets done properly. Like with my albums and Yoko's, each time I have to go through the same process: check if it was sent to so-and-so. Did this happen? Get the printing size right. I want it clear and simple and all that. Like for an advert. I have to go through the same jazz all the time. It's never a lesson learned.

Int.: Let's get back to talking about the group, and the four different personalities involved. When we've asked about the split, people give many different reasons for it. Neil Aspinall, your old Liverpool friend and managing director of Apple, said you were like guys going through war on those tours, and when you came back, you found out you were very different people. I asked Lee Eastman for his view of the split, and what it was that prompted Paul to file suit to dissolve the Beatles' partnership, and he said it was because John asked for a divorce.

John: Because I asked for a divorce? That's a childish reason for going into court, isn't it? Have you talked to Lee Eastman for your book?

Int.: Yes.

John: Did he get angry and yell at you?

Int.: He got pretty heated once on the phone.

John: Good; that shows I'm not making it up. Because I'm the only one who's ever talked about it.

Int.: What was it like for you when the court case was on, with all the publicity?

John: Well, when it first started, I got on a boat and went to Japan for two weeks, and nobody could get in touch with me. They got me in Miami, then I got to Japan and I didn't tell anybody I'd arrived. We just pissed off up in the hills and nobody could find us. Then suddenly I get these calls from the lawyer, fucking idiot. I didn't like his voice, as soon as I heard him, you know. A sort of upper-class Irish-English voice. Fuck. And then he insisted I come home. I could have done it all on the fucking phone. And I came home and we were having meetings all the time with these counsels, every other day, and it went on for weeks and weeks. George and Ringo were getting restless and didn't want to do it anymore. And then George would say, "I've had enough. I don't want to do it. Fuck it all. I don't care if I'm poor." George goes through that every now and then. "I'll give it all away." Will he fuck? He's got it all charted up, like monopoly money.

Int.: Let's talk a bit about George. He's perhaps the most enigmatic Beatle. Are you saying George is more conventional than he makes himself out to be?

John: There's no telling George. He always has a point of view about *that* wide, you know. [John places his hands a few inches apart.] You can't tell him anything.

Yoko: George is sophisticated, fashionwise....

John: He's very trendy, and he has the right clothes, and all of that....

Yoko: But he's not sophisticated, intellectually.

John: No. He's very narrow-minded and he doesn't really have a broader view. Paul is far more aware than George. One time in the Apple office in Wigmore Street, I said something to George, and he said, "I'm as intelligent as you, you know." This must have been resentment, but he could have left anytime if I was giving him a hard time.

Int.: What did you say?

John: I didn't answer. Of course, he's got an inferiority complex working with Paul and me.

Yoko: In the case of Paul, it's not that he's not sophisticated. I'm sure that he's intellectually sophisticated as well. It's just that he's aware, and yet he doesn't want to know.

John: Whereas George doesn't really know what's happening, you know.

Int.: Did it ever strike you after meeting Yoko that you could get from her the intellectual tussle that you couldn't get from your "mates."

John: Yeah.

Int.: How were your thought processes working at that time?

John: Toward being able to relate to a woman you mean?

Int.: Yes.

Yoko: I forget who it was, but someone said

that the only thinking person in England is John Lennon—and that's my feeling. Because among the Beatles, you know, the only person who's even aware of the female-lib thing, and all that, is John. So I couldn't really speak with or talk to any of them, except John.

John: Well, they don't listen to women. Women are chicks to them.

Yoko: And John is really in the present time, you know. Whereas the others in many ways, in so many ways, are still in Liverpool, you know. The only one who is sophisticated enough to talk equally with intellectuals and all that is John. Really. That's why I can talk to him, and it makes me feel very good, you know.

John: I'm glad about that.

Int.: So let's talk about you and John. A man called John Donbar introduced you, didn't he?

John: Yeah. He brought us together, so I'll always have a soft spot for him.

Yoko: And he didn't even introduce me to John as ... what I mean is, he didn't say, "This is John Lennon," or anything like that. So I didn't know it was John.

Int.: So, John. How long did it take you to realize that Yoko might be able to offer you a lot?

John: Well, of course, when I first saw her art-gallery show, that was a bit of an eye-opener. I wasn't quite sure what it was about. I knew there was some sort of con game going on somewhere. She calls herself a concept artist, but with the "cept" off, it's con artist. I saw that side of it, and that was interesting, and then we met.

Yoko: Every artist is a concept artist, I'm a con artist.

Int.: Was it love at first sight?

John: Well, I always had this dream of meeting an artist woman that I would fall in love with. Even from art school. And when we met and were talking, I just realized that she knew everything I knew and more probably. And it was coming out of a woman's head. It just sort of bowled me over. It was like finding gold or something. To find something that you could go and get pissed with, and to have exactly the same relationship with any mate in Liverpool you'd ever had, but also you could go to bed with it, and it could stroke your head when you felt tired or sick or depressed. Could also be mother. Obviously, with the male-female thing, you can take those roles with each other. And if the intellect is there, if it's compatible, well, it's just like winning the pools, you know. So that's why when people ask me for a précis of my story, I put, "Born, lived, met Yoko," because that's what it's been about.

Int.: And when did all this hit home?

John: I can't remember. She was coming on, and as she was talking to me, I would get high, and the discussion would get to such a level that I would be going higher and higher. And when she'd leave, I'd go back to this sort of suburbia. Then I'd meet her again and my head would go off like I was on an acid trip. And I'd be going over what she said, and it was incredible, some of the ideas and the way she was saying them. It was turning me on, you know. And then once I'd got a sniff of it, I was hooked. Then I couldn't leave her alone. We couldn't be apart for a minute from then on. And we just moved in together—that was it.

Yoko: He has this nature, and I'm thankful for it. The thing is, most men are so narrow-minded. Somebody once told me ... I don't make small talk, and that's why men hate you. I mean, I have so many male enemies who try to stifle me. What the hell.

John: I did the same of course . . .

Yoko: Why do they hate me because I don't make small talk?

John: . . . See, I found myself being a chauvinist pig with her. I didn't know I was, but then I started thinking, "Well, if I said that to Paul, or asked Paul to do that, or George, or Ringo, they'd tell me to fuck off." And then you start to realize: you just sort of have this attitude to women, which is just insane! It's like an attitude to blacks! It's just beyond belief, the way we're brought up to think of women. And I had to keep saying, "Well, would I tell a guy to do that? Would I say that to a guy? Would a guy take that?" Then I started getting nervous. I thought, "Fuck, I better treat her right or she's going to go. No friend's going to stick around for this kind of treatment."

Int.: In the early stages of the group's career, you all seemed to trade off each other, and play off each other's jokes, and it was fairly obvious you all got along well. You all seemed close, and there was an evident togetherness among you. Did that break down for you when you met Yoko?

John: Well, it had broken down before that. There was this Liverpool thing, and everyone who worked for us was from Liverpool, and so there was that. But that togetherness had gone a long time before Yoko. We were really all on our own.

Int.: Wasn't it true, though, that there was a kind of esprit de corps among you all, a kind of machismo thing about all being together.

John: Yeah, but that ennoblement of being together had worn off. It had ended. After *Sergeant Pepper*, or round about *Pepper*, it was wearing off. There was no longer any spark. All Yoko did was rekindle whatever it was in me . . . the creative urge.

Yoko: You were writing "I Am the Walrus," and you just showed me parts of it. Maybe you don't remember this . . . but you just suddenly . . .

Int.: When you first met John, Yoko, did you know anything about rock music?

Yoko: I didn't know anything about pop music. I didn't know anything about rock, or anything like it. I just realized it was a sort of poetry. I thought of pop songs as something a bit lower than poetry. It was like reading Dylan Thomas-type poetry, that had

"The reason I got rich is because I'm so insecure. I'm not secure enough to give it all up, because I need it to protect me from whatever I'm frightened of." *Michael Brennan © Scope Features*

PRESS CONFERENCE TO ANNOUNCE THE FORMATION OF APPLE (1968). "Although Apple turned into the Beatles' baby, Apple was conceived by the Epsteins and NEMS before we took over, before we said: 'It's going to be like this.' They had it lined up so we would do the same as Northern Songs, sell ourselves to ourselves." © *Raeanne Rubenstein*

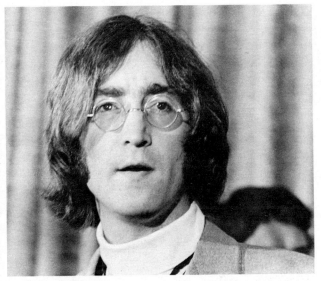

"The haircuts—many art students I'd seen for ten years before had had the haircut. We made it famous, that's all." © *Raeanne Rubenstein*

A BIRTHDAY PARTY FOR JOHN IN 1971
(*right, clapping, Allen Ginsberg; front left, with
guitar, Phil Spector*). "I think the most
important thing the Beatles did was to show the
kids that you don't have to be born an
aristocrat . . . You can make it young . . . You can
make it working class." © *Raeanne Rubenstein*

"The Beatle togetherness had gone a long time before Yoko. We were really all on our own, just living in separate vacuums." *David Spindel*

JOHN WITH HIS FIRST SON, JULIAN. "I'm not the easiest guy to read, although I'm fairly naive and open in some ways. I can be conned easily. But in other ways I'm quite complicated, and it's not easy to get through all the defenses and see what I'm like." *Michael Brennan © Scope Features*

"Well, I thought, I can't really go on the road and take a lot of money. A) What am I going to do with it? And B) How could I look somebody in the eye? Why should they pay? I've got everything I need." *Michael Brennan © Scope Features*

"I was getting into that established, fat, professional-pop-star-can-do-no-wrong, worker genius, a record every few months, and that's all right. A few Hare Krishnas here and there, and I've done my social bit." *Michael Brennan © Scope Features*

"I never knew what I wanted in a woman. I knew I wanted someone intelligent or someone arty . . . I always had this dream of meeting an artist woman that I would fall in love with."

Yoko: "Every artist is a concept artist. I'm a con artist."
© *Raeanne Rubenstein*

"I like to dress Yoko and present her."

© Raeanne Rubenstein

Yoko: "I used to despise every man that I met. I'm real female lib, and the rest of the Beatles, aside from Ringo who's been very good, showed their true colors by completely ignoring me in public." © *Raeanne Rubenstein*

John: "It was always presumed that Yoko would join me, and that I didn't need to do anything. That's why I changed my name to Ono, to show people." © *Raeanne Rubenstein*

John: "Normally I would win an argument, whether I was right or wrong, especially if the argument was with a woman—they'd just give in.

And Yoko didn't. She'd go on and on and on, until I understood it. Then I had to treat her with respect."

© Raeanne Rubenstein

Yoko: "To communicate with people is almost a responsibility. We are living proof of East and West getting along together." *David Spindel*

a delicate kind of metric rhythm to it. And I thought, "Oh, my gosh, he's a poet." And I was very surprised.

Int.: Were you kind of looking down your nose at rock?

John: She didn't even think about it.

Yoko: Well, I went to his recording session, you know. And the Beatles were going one, two, three, four; one, two, three, four. And I'm used to Rayburn and Berg, things like that. . . .

John: She thought it was very childish.

Yoko: Very childish.

John: She used to say, "Why are you doing that same beat all the time?" I used to get very irritated by her intellectual attitude. I have the same feeling about art, you know.

Int.: What were your feelings about art and the art world at this time?

John: Well, I went to art school and I thought that was the art world, virtually. And they're all such pretentious hypocrites. And there were no artists I admired, except for maybe Dali, or some artists from the past. But I always read the art reviews in *The Times* and the *Observer*. And when I read the art reviews, I always had this feeling, "Well, why aren't I in them?" You know that thing, when you're not actually doing it. So I couldn't understand why I wasn't being reviewed for my art, because I always felt like an artist. And it was silly. Or it was like reading literary supplements, and wondering why they're not talking about you when you haven't got a book out. A strange thing. So I really despised art and artists, because they're all hypocrites and they're all phoney, and they're all upper-class. There wasn't any working-class artist, really. And it was all bullshit and phoney.

So I went to her show, and I was thinking, "Fucking artist shit. It's all bullshit." But then there were so many good jokes in it, real good eye-openers.

Yoko: That's another thing: most artists don't have a sense of humor.

John: And there *was* a sense of humor in her work, you know. It was funny. Her work really made me laugh, some of it. So that's when I got interested in art again, just through her work.

Yoko: Also, my art is street art. But to talk about men: all the men I met, I felt they were more pretentious than me, hypocritical, narrower than me, and not genuine. And I'm talented. Because I can compose,

I can paint, I can be in many fields. Whereas most men that I met were bragging about their professionalism in one field.

John: They get one idea and flog it to death, and become famous on one idea.

Yoko: And fucking conservative, you know. They have no sense of humor, and they talk about women not having a sense of humor. I thought they had less humor than me. So I used to despise every man that I met. I was thinking, "There's something wrong with me," because everybody hated me for it. Because ... well, they just hated me for it, so I thought there must be something wrong.

And then I met this man, and for the first time I got the fright of my life because here was a man who was just as genuine, maybe more genuine, than me. He's very genuine. And he can do anything that I can do, which is very unusual, I felt. And I really got surprised. And that happened at the first meeting. It was almost like fate that he came into the gallery. Like if I wrote a novel about it, people would think, "It's too fictitious, this sort of thing doesn't happen," but in some ways it was too symbolic for words. Like I had this hammer-and-nail painting, right. And it was virginal—nobody had put a nail in it yet. And he came in before the opening, and he asked if he could hammer a nail in. Now that's very symbolic, isn't it? And also, there was another thing he saw, a painting on the ceiling ...

John: That was the first thing I saw.

Yoko: ... You climb up a ladder. You take a magnifying glass and you look at it, and it's a ceiling painting, a tiny, tiny, little word that says "Yes." And it's almost like I said yes to him.

John: Most of the artists were saying "no," or "hee-hee-hee," or "fuck off." Whatever the art was, the modern art, it was always "fuck off." This one said "yes." So that's the reason I stayed at the show and saw the rest of it. And then she said, "Well, give me five bob to knock a nail in." So I said, "Well, I'll give you an imaginary five shillings and then hammer an imaginary nail in." Which is her whole trip. I didn't know about it, because I was from Liverpool. All I'd ever heard of was Van Gogh.

Yoko: So I said, "My God, he's playing the same game I'm playing. And then later I thought, "How symbolic that is, that I said 'yes' to him—not in social conversation, but way up there." Weird, isn't it? So it was a whole trip, even for cynics like us. Well, cynics are usually the most naïve people, inside. So we just sort of naïvely fell for each other.

Int.: Did you feel immediately that you suited each other?

Yoko: It was good. I think I'd seen myself as arty, middle-class ... that sort of thing. ...

John: ... And I was getting into that established, fat, professional-pop-star-can-do-no-wrong, worker genius, a record every few months thing, and that's all right. A few Hare Krishnas here and there, and I've done my social bit. And she was a sort of pretentious, avant-garde, this-is-all-that's-happening-in-the-world, middle-class ...

Yoko: Snob.

John: ... Snob. And we beat the fuck out of each other until we got rid of it. I mean verbally.

Yoko: It was very good for both of us.

John: It took me a long time to get used to it. Any woman I could shout down. Most of my arguments, with anybody, used to be a question of who could shout the loudest. Normally I would win the argument, whether I was right or wrong, especially if the argument was with a woman—they'd just give in. And she didn't. She'd go on and on and on, until I understood it. Then I had to treat her with respect.

Yoko: So this was a good basis for your relationship?

John: Yeah. Right. And I'd never had a relationship before then, because before then everything else had been sort of an unnatural relationship. Because before then they'd all been the usual ... So I was very surprised.

Yoko: I think relationships are usually made out of convenience, and not out of respect. And therefore I think they're rare.

Int.: Yoko, let me ask you this. During the time that your relationship with John was forming, what was the attitude of the rest of the Beatles, and the Beatle entourage, toward you?

Yoko: Well, I'm real female lib, and the rest of the Beatles, aside from Ringo who's been very good, showed their true colors by completely ignoring me in public.

John: That's when I saw their colors for the first time.

Yoko: Can you imagine it? I'm a woman who

supposedly came into their world ... to that extend I had some influence on them. But they would never speak of me in public, never mention anything, in any article. And presumably reporters would ask them about me.

John: ....Ask about all the things they did to Yoko from the beginning. They don't know it because they do it naturally. They don't know, because they're men. I *really* think they don't know because they're men. They treated her like they would treat any woman. Just tell him, Yoko, the things that Derek [Derek Taylor started out in the Beatle entourage as Brian Epstein's assistant, handled Beatle PR, and became one of their retainers and closest associates during the Apple phase] would do in the beginning ... because I didn't know. And she kept telling me: "Derek is doing this, and Derek is doing that," and I said, "You're paranoid." And we took him on the bed event, and she kept saying, "Don't bring him, I don't want him here," because when it came to any publicity ... I mean, even now in Apple, they sometimes miss Yoko's records off a listing, or if they give it to *New Musical Express*, they give them the wrong one. There's always something wrong. One of Yoko's albums will be missing, or they'll have got it mixed up. And after the *Look* magazine article, when this old friend of Yoko's really shat on her, Derek came up to me and said: "Well, at least they didn't shit on you, John." Meaning that's all right, you know. They had nothing to say about you, John. Don't worry.

He [Derek] was one of them who wanted the Beatles to carry on because it was his gravy train, the same with Neil and Mal, and all them. [Neil Aspinall and Mal Evans were both key members of the Beatles' entourage.] You tell them the things that actually happened.

Yoko: With any human being I feel I want to be just to them. This is a a kick I have . . . a thing I have because of my upbringing. I want to be a good girl. So with Derek, I came on straight with him. And in Montreux, in Switzerland, when we went to this film festival, I said, "Listen. You're a good writer, supposedly. So if you're a good writer, that means you have pride as an artist. So why don't you really try to write something good. Now you're being an assistant to us. Why is that? It's a very passive role. And you all are being rich men's chauffeurs, and that's no way to be creative. You cannot be creative as long as you're a rich man's chauffeur. You have to speak for yourself. You have to write something. You have to do something on your own. Otherwise you can't have any respect for yourself. And if you don't have any respect for yourself, what kind of a relationship are you going to have with John? It's just going to be one of resentment. . . .

John: Because he was always hinting: "What kind of a job is this?" And he wished he could go write his book, and all that. And I'd always say, "Well, go write your fucking book." So in a way he was resenting us, like people do, like chauffeurs do, in a way: "I could have been a famous writer if I wasn't polishing your shoes." Well, stop doing it, and go and do it.

Yoko: Or I could have been a famous painter if I didn't marry this guy for love, as my mother used to say—

John: Go on then. Get to the point.

Yoko: So I said that to Derek. And I also said: "If you carry resentment subconsciously, then when you are talking to us nicely that means you are being a hypocrite. And that's no good. The only way to stop your resentment is to do your own work, you know, do something that is yours." So I thought I was being on the level by saying that, and then the next thing he tells a reporter that Yoko says, 'We are all rich men's chauffeurs, including herself,' and it was written up. And that's a snide remark, and that's bad.

Int.: You have pretty strong reactions toward people who downplay the importance of your work.

Yoko: Well, another thing was, when I was busy working at Apple, and really busy, okay, doing four interviews, that kind of thing, there was this attitude of, "You know, Yoko, you don't have to do all these things. You are Mrs. Lennon." I said, "Would you say the same thing to John? That he doesn't have to do his art? You would never say that to John." They were saying, "Why did I have to be creative, why did I have to do all these things?"

Int.: So they, the other Beatles and the Apple entourage, they wanted you to stay quiet.

John: Yeah, that's what they wanted, all of them.

Yoko: It's like they're saying that my art is not as important as John's art, right? That's an outright insult. You don't say that to anybody, even if you think it, right? That's a male chauvinist statement.

Another thing was, one time we were in a car, big Beatles scene and all, and John said: "So I come from Liverpool, the big Beatles scene, and all that, and Yoko comes from the East and the West, a completely different environment. She was a New York artist," and so forth. . . . And they said, "Right, and now she has to learn the ways of the Beatles, and she now has to join their family and become one of us." But the point is, why should I become one of them? Why shouldn't John and I meet in the middle? Why do I have to come into his life? He came into my life too.

John: Right, right. It was always presumed that she'd join me, and that I didn't need to do anything. That's why I changed me name to Ono, to show people, you know? It was just exactly the same for me as her. And Derek, and Neil and all them . . . chauvinists . . . chauffeurs . . . resented the fact that she wasn't going to join in . . .

Yoko: Their attitude was, nothing should be changed. Come on as an obedient little girl . . .

John: . . . Just behave like Cyn and Pattie [George's wife] and all them, go in the background. . . .

Yoko: Then it's all right, but otherwise we can't accept you. We're not going to change anything for her. She has to change. That bit. Join the family. And I'm in love with John, and I have no intention of joining the family.

So, there was a reporter who came, and he wanted John for *World in Action*—it's a program on TV. And I was an artist before I met John, and whenever I had a chance, like at a cocktail party or any place, I would hustle my work. I never went to a cocktail party without thinking that I should really hustle my work, because I was a dedicated artist, you know? And I really felt good about pushing my art, doing something good for the world, through my art . . . like the Black Bag thing . . .

John: Well, whatever . . . get on with it.

Yoko: . . . So the thing is, whenever I meet anybody for the first time, I'd say, "All right, why don't you put me on your program?" So this guy comes in and says, "I want John Lennon for the program," and I said: "Okay, why don't you have me as well? And let me show my art in it." And Derek was there, and he just went, "Oh, my God, my God!" and he was saying so I could hear: "Fuck, if she's going to come on that aggressive and go on the show, it's not going to work. That's the end. It's not going to work. Don't worry about it, you don't have to do it." That's what he was saying to the guy. But the point is, what the hell is that? I mean, it's very important and natural for me to come on with "how about my art?" And they took it that I was using John, which wasn't the case. In any circumstances I would always have come out with those statements.

John: So, anyway, these are just the statements Derek made. But that was their whole attitude to Yoko at the office, which Derek was like kingpin of. And that was it all the time. They'd miss her off the lists of records. They would never help her in any way, they always hindered her. And Paul, and Derek, and all of them were in collusion to kill *Two Virgins*. I was told by people who had meetings ... they had *meetings* where Paul said, "Let's kill it," after he wrote about two great saints on the fucking front, and all that. So all that was going on, and I gave 'em chance after chance. I said, "Look, they'll get used to it, they'll get used to it." And they went on and on and on, just being abusive, and being like that, and trying to pretend that she didn't exist and that she didn't have any art, that she had a lucky break meeting me, and that she should be on her fucking knees, and not interfere with them. But she'd stand up to them and say, "That's dumb! What the hell do you want to do that for? You don't do that to John Lennon. Leave him alone." Or, "That's not the kind of way to treat him, push him, or whatever." And she'd start telling them, as an equal, what she thought about any given situation. And they couldn't take it.

Int.: Was it a lesson learned, eventually?

John: No.

Int.: After you gave an interview once, Taylor said he was sad you felt this way.

John: Well, that's that game they play. Neil Aspinall plays that game too. At one point, in one of the Northern Songs proceedings, I sent a telegram to Neil, because I'd heard he'd been doing things behind me back, and I said: "Don't bite the hand that feeds you." Because I was the one that protected him many times from Paul. Paul had no love for Neil, and vice versa. And all of a sudden he's a Paul man. Because they clung to Paul—Derek included—because they all thought Paul was the one who was going to hold it all together. So they had a choice of which side to come down on, and they chose Paul, and the past, and at that moment I cut 'em off.

You see, they get under the delusion that they are the Beatles. They begin to think that they are the Beatles, that they are the source of power.

Int.: They do tend to talk about "we" all the time.

John: I know! "*We* took acid!" "We" took acid!

Yoko: I tried to be friendly with them. I mean, without coming into the family bit, I tried to be family as well, in a way. So, for instance, I told Paul—I said, "Paul, please understand this. If Linda gets a prize in filmmaking or photography, because that's her thing, we're all going to be proud. It's going to be good for the Beatles, good for all of us, and I would be proud of it, because she's one of the family." I said, "I was an artist. I was working very hard until I met John. Please let me work. And obviously, you know it's very difficult for me to work now, the way it is. I'm suffocated. Please just have some kindness and let me work, make it easier for me to work, or help me. We should all help each other."

So then the next day he said: "You know, the doctor said you should really not be vegetarian or macrobiotic, you should really start eating meat." Linda and I had the same doctor. And I said, "What?" So then he said, "You just told me we should help each other, so I'm just giving you information."

He really didn't understand. I meant help me in my work. So he really didn't mean badly, but he really didn't understand. Because at one point I said, "Listen, I'm so much in love with John. Sometimes because I'm so involved in his work, I feel like forgetting about my work. How's that? I'm a real masochist now." And he said, "Right, that's good. You feel happy with that. That's women's happiness." He believed that. And he encouraged me to forget about my work, and said, "Listen, be in the background. As long as you're in the background, in the long run that's better for you too. So he really wanted to make a wife out of me, you know?

Int.: Let's talk a bit about your lives in New York. Both you and Paul have spent a lot of time here recently, and come under a different type of scrutiny. Paul's more secluded, but I read they were demonstrating outside Eastman's house last week.

John: Oh, yeah. It was on TV. About Paul. Paul's dead and all that. It's A. J. Webermann and all those people. I hope they're not after me. I think it's funny as shit. Paul said to me on the phone, "Well, I'm the rebel now, and I'm enjoying it." He thinks that's a rebel.

Int.: I see the rock press has taken a few cuts at you too. A story I read by Lillian Roxon—

John: Well, Lillian starts writing that I'm going around trying to get into the New York art scene, sort of humbling myself, chasing after every great name from Warhol onwards. She wrote a piece like that. And it all came from this trick tape I made saying, "What a shame Andy isn't here, isn't it? Isn't it a pity Andy's not here?" Every ten minutes I'd say it. And it's obvious to anybody that I'm camping it. It's so obvious. And Lillian says I'm crawling, that I can't think of anything else but Warhol. And pushing my way in to all the celebrities of New York. It just happens that Yoko knows every fucker in New York who ever was anybody. And she introduced them to me. That's all.

Yoko: Old friends of mine.

Int.: But you once told me, John, that you admire Lillian Roxon's book, *Rock Encyclopedia.*

John: Oh, very intelligent book that. I thought that was the most precise history of rock and roll I've ever read, with the influence of Elvis upon me, upon Dylan, the influence of Dylan upon us, and us upon Dylan. There was very little she got wrong. That's the first time I've ever read a real review of the whole rock scene where the influences are right.

Int.: Did you ever notice who the book is dedicated to?

John: Who is it dedicated to?

Int.: Linda Eastman. Because Linda had a big friendship with Lillian.

John: Well, I didn't know that.

Int.: So how do you react, John, when you're chastised in print?

John: I don't know. I don't mind people attacking me, but . . .

Int.: Do you hate it if it happens all the time?

John: Well, people have told me to forget about it and not to bother. I mean, with Lillian it's just silly because I know she's intelligent. And then of course, things get repeated. Like *Disc* picks it up . . . which is another paper that hates us . . . and it looks like I'm running around, and doing too much and all that shit. It was terrible, the repercussions, just because she wrote that. Of course, it doesn't really matter, and I'll last out longer than Lillian Roxon probably, so what's the use?

Yoko: Jerry Rubin wrote something about John, without knowing John. And now that Jerry's met John, he's embarrassed. He said, "Listen, I didn't know that John was such a great guy."

Int.: So, Yoko, let's switch subjects. John's been finding out about your New York world, but did you have any idea of what the Beatles' life had been like, on the tours, for example?

John: She was really shocked. I thought the art world was loose, you know? And when I started telling her about what our life was like, she couldn't believe it. But since then she's been asking her old friends. She thought nobody knew about the Beatles [scene], and then after talking to a few old friends of hers who I've got close to, I find out they knew all about the Beatles. They knew all about the raving. They were into raving. She was like this silly Eastern nun wandering about, thinking it was all spiritual.

Int.: I guess it was hardly that.

John: Oh, yeah. Fielding didn't stand a chance alongside all that shit.

Yoko: So thank God, I was in the art world, and I'm so old ...

John: She's saying thank God, she wasn't a raver.

Yoko: So nobody has anything on me.

John: Well, we didn't tell you about chapter four, about the orgy at the avant-garde festival in 1922.

Yoko: I mean, I come from a different generation. My friends didn't want me to know they smoked pot, you know. They were always hiding the pot from me. So, anyway, I thought, "He's an artist. He's probably had two or three affairs. And then I heard the whole story, and I thought, "My God!"

I mean, he once said to me, "Well, were you a groupie in the art world?" I said, "What's a groupie?"

John: I said, "Just tell me. I don't want to go round, and fucking Picasso or somebody comes up and says, "Yes, we've had her.' "

Yoko: And I really didn't know the word "groupie."

John: So anyway, I'd been dying to tell her about the raving on tour for years, you know, because I just wanted people to know what a scene it was. I thought it was silly not to say anything. And I had to choose between just sort of saying it, and maybe hurting people, you know, and finally I just thought, fuck it. I didn't go into detail, but I just let it be known that it was some kind of scene on the road, and that's why people like Neil, they were living like kings, you know. They were having more fun than us. We were locked in our rooms all the time. They were going to the whorehouses and ordering up the class whores. We were locked in our fucking room, and we couldn't go out. So they were living like fucking emperors, and that's why they were clinging to the past so much.

Int.: Do you resent it that so many people seem to take credit for their contribution to the Beatles?

John: Well, I read an article about Derek the other day by a guy who was hustling us in Toronto, and he was saying, "If John Lennon hadn't been there, Derek Taylor would have been the great wit, or whatever, shit like that . . .

Yoko: But what did he do?

John: . . . But it's like Allen says, "What has George Martin, or Derek, or any of these people done since we dropped them?" Now George Martin—there's an article on him in *Melody Maker*, and he's telling all these stories. He's fairly accurate ... he's quite interesting—so anyway, they start one of these stories off with "John Lennon says, 'What has George Martin written?'" And then they try and justify what he did in the past. He says, "Well, I put these loops together, I showed him how to play feedback," or put loops together, or some arbitrary little technical thing, like showing you how to lay a page out, you know. So the fact is, what has Derek done? Where's this book he's writing? Where is the great talent of George Martin and Derek Taylor, and the legacy of Brian Epstein? Show me some of their work and I'll start believing these stories. George Martin has never produced anything in his life! Well, Seatrain, whatever. But musically, they almost intimate that *he wrote everything*.

Yoko: It's like my ex-husband saying that he sacrificed his talent for me. He's done nothing. What did he do after that?

John: Well, I never had anything against George Martin, and he is doing well. I just didn't like all those rumors that he actually was the brains behind the Beatles. I can't stand that.

Int.: We talked recently to the man who produced *Yellow Submarine*, Al Brodax, and he said categorically that George Martin was half of everything the Beatles ever recorded.

John: Oh, that's bullshit. You know what Brodax used to do? Brodax got half the *Yellow Submarine* out of my mouth. You know the idea for the Hoover? The machine that sucks people up? All those were my ideas. They used to come to the studio and sort of chat ... "Hi, John, old bean. Got any ideas for the film?" And I'd just spout out all this stuff, and they went off and did it, you know. Brodax probably thinks that because Brian made a mistake by letting George Martin put in all those fills in *Yellow Submarine*, the "Sea of Holes" shit. And he recorded all this terrible shit that went out with our LP, you know. If you'd check it out, it's a whole sort of joke: George Martin is on one side of our album. Oh, we didn't notice that.

Yoko: But you know, it's amazing. I'm referred to as a Japanese actress or something, and my ex-husband, Tony Cox, who has never made a film in his life, who just sort of helped *me* make a film, is called the filmmaker.

John: Yeah, he's always referred to as the producer-director, and they still call her actress.

Yoko: It's really unfair. And the world is so male chauvinist, it's amazing. I mean if *I* only made one film, or didn't have anything to do with a film, but just help on it, nobody's going to call *me* a filmmaker.

Int.: So, John, of all the early influences on the Beatles that *were* important, which would you say had the greatest effect on the group. Was it Liverpool? The Cavern? Hamburg? Did Hamburg really improve the playing?

John: Oh, amazingly. Because before that we'd only been playing bits and pieces, but in Hamburg we had to play for hours and hours on end.

Int.: Let's talk a bit about the Hamburg days, because obviously those experiences took place before the group had any kind of renown. How did you feel when Alan Williams sent you over there, and you wound up on the Reeperbahn?

John: Well, we auditioned for it, and we had no drummer. We just had a stand-in drummer for the day. And Stu [Sutcliffe] couldn't play bass, so he had to turn his back. So we got there ... Alan Williams took us over in a van. We went through Holland, and did a bit of shoplifting there, and then we arrived in Hamburg and were put in this sort of pigsty, like a toilet in a cinema it was, a rundown sort of flea pit. And we were living in a toilet, like right next to the ladies' toilet.

And so [laughs] we'd wake up in the morning, and the films would be on, and there would be old German fraus pissing next door. That was where we washed. That was our bathroom. So it was a bit of a shock in a way.

Int.: How much touring or playing experience did you have up to then?

John: Well, we'd done the Johnny Gentle tour, but we'd only been on stage for a bit. We'd only been on for twenty minutes or so, because he'd been on most of the time. But with this thing we had to play all the tunes for hours and hours on end. That's why every song lasted twenty minutes and had twenty solos in it. We'd be playing eight or ten hours a night or something. And that's what improved the playing. And also, the Germans like heavy rock, you know, so we had to really keep rocking all the time, and that's how we got stomping. And it was all four in a bar, because the drummer, Pete Best, could only do four in the bar on his bass drum, so everything we did was just boom, boom, boom, boom, like that. So that's how it developed, and that of course made the sound, because we developed a sound by playing hours and hours and hours together.

Int.: You found yourself playing in unbelievably bad conditions.

John: Yeah, but it was still rather thrilling when you went on stage. It was a little nightclub. And it was a bit frightening because it wasn't a dance hall, and all these people were sitting down, expecting something. And then they would want us to "mak show" and of course whenever there was any pressure point, I had to get us out of it. They always said, "Well, okay, John, you're the leader." When nothing was going on, they'd say, "Uh-uh, no leader, fuck it." But if anything happened, it was like, "Okay, you're the leader, you get up and do a show." So I had to get up, and I played fucking Gene Vincent for three weeks. The second night they said, "The first night you were terrible, you have to make a show—'mak show.'" So I put me guitar down and I did Gene Vincent all night, you know, banging and lying on the floor, and throwing the mike around, and pretending that I had a bad leg. That was some experience. So the Germans kept saying "mak show, mak show," and then the police closed down the first club because we were too loud. It was right at the end of the Reeperbahn, well, not the Reeperbahn but the other little street that goes off it, I can't remember the name of it. I remember we were nearly in the housing district.

Then he moved us to his other club, which was larger, and where they danced. There was more dance space. And beer tables. And there was another group. Then they brought Howie Casey over, or Ringo— I think it was Howie Casey first—or maybe they were even there when we got there. But anyway, they were playing at the other club, this guy's club. And they were pretty competent. They had saxes, and they were really a together group. They had a black singer who couldn't really sing, but he was a real showman. So we had to compete with them at first, and we had to start putting on this show, to compete, to get enough people in our club, even though they were owned by the same person. Then they moved us in with them—Rorie Stone, and Ringo—they were professionals. We were still amateurs. They'd been going for years, and they'd been to Butlins, and God-knows-what, and they really knew how to put on a show. So we had to compete with those two then, and that's how we started "mak-ing show," and we'd all end up jumping around on the floor ... Paul would be doing "What I Say?" for an hour and a half ... they're all into it now, lying on the floor and banging your guitar and kicking things, and just doing all that jazz, to keep 'em happy.

And we'd always be drunk because all these gangsters would come in, like the local Mafia. They'd send a crate of champagne onstage, this imitation German champagne, and we had to drink it or they'd kill us [laughs], you know. They'd say, "Drink it," then do "What I Say?" So then they'd get us pissed, and we'd have to do this show for them. Whatever time of night they came in, if they came in at five in the morning and we'd been playing seven hours, they'd give us a crate of champagne and we were supposed to carry on. And then we'd get pills off the waiters, to keep awake and to stop being drunk as well. So that's how it all started.

I used to be so pissed ... I'd be lying on the stage floor behind the piano, drunk, while the rest of the group was playing. I'd just be on stage fast asleep. And then we always ate on stage, too, because we never had time to eat. So it was a real scene ...

it would be a far-out show now, they'd think, "What a far-out show," eating and smoking and swearing and going to sleep on stage when you were tired. And some shows I went on just in me underpants—this was in later shows at the larger club, the Star Club, when Gerry and the Pacemakers and the whole of Liverpool was over there. And we'd really get going then. I'd go on in me underpants, and with a toilet seat round me neck, and all sorts of gear on. And OUT OF ME FUCKING MIND. And I'd do a drum solo, which I couldn't do, 'cause I couldn't play drums, while Gerry Marsden was playing.

There's all big exaggerated stories about us in Hamburg, about us pissing on nuns and things like that, but there was a lot of things that went on. What actually happened with that [the nun's episode] was one morning—see, we had a balcony later on in these flats—and one Sunday morning we were all just pissing in the street as all the people were going to church. And there were some nuns over the road, going into the church. It was just a Sunday morning in the club district, with everyone walking about, and three or four people just peeing into the street. So we were always doing gigs like that, and everyone was always stabbing—everybody had knives—and was always breaking up the furniture. Just really wild scenes, it was.

Int.: Did you ever want to give it all up?

John: Oh, no. Well, obviously, if you'd only had two hours sleep, and then you'd have to wake up and take a pill, and it would be going on and on and on, and since you didn't get a day off, then you'd just begin to go out of your mind with tiredness. And then you'd think you'd be glad to get out of there. But then you'd go back to Liverpool, and you'd only remember the good fun you had in Hamburg, so you wouldn't mind going back. But after the last time, we really didn't want to go back, when Brian made us go back to fulfill the contract. If we'd had our way, we'd have just copped out on the engagement, because we didn't feel we owed them fuck all. I mean, we made all those clubs into international clubs.

It was the same with the *Merseybeat*, you know, [The *Merseybeat* was Liverpool's rock and roll newspaper.] and all those newspaper people. Newspaper people have the habit of putting you on the front page to sell their papers, and then after they've sold their papers and got big circulations, they say, "Look what we've done for you." The *Merseybeat* was a nonexistent rag until we got big in Hamburg, came back, and were on the front page. And that's how they sold. They put us on every week. The kids didn't want to know about any other group in Liverpool. So we made the paper.

Also, I wrote for the paper, and all that. I'd like you to trace them if you can, I can't find the originals. Some of the things went into *In His Own Write* and I've got them all except one called "Small Sam," about a guy with a clubfoot, or rather, a club-you-grow-you-quickly shoe. And I used to write a thing called "Beatcomber," because I admired the column "Beach-comber" in the *Daily Express*. So I used to write this column, and then they asked me to write the story of the Beatles. And that's when I wrote with George "a man came on a flaming pie" because even then they were asking, "How did you get the name Beatles?" Bill Harry said, "Look, they're always asking you how you got the name Beatles. Why don't you tell 'em how you got the name?" So I wrote: "There was an certain man, and he came ..." —I was still doing like, from school, all this imitation Bible stuff— "... and he came, and said you are Beatles with an 'a' ... and man came on a flaming pie from the sky, and said you are Beatles with an 'a.'

And thence they were. And forthcoming there was a drummer of great renown and five foot high ..." and all that kind of jazz.

Int.: So, let's talk more about your manager, your first manager, Brian Epstein. What did you think of Brian?

John: Well, he was all right. I've found out since, of course, that he wasn't quite as honest to us as he made out.

Int.: How do you mean?

John: Well, because ... Well, I think Dick James and them might have carved him up a bit, you know. But Brian definitely looked after himself and not us. NEMS [Epstein's company] was in a good position at the end, wasn't it? Wasn't it us having to buy NEMS out? NEMS ended up a strong company. The Beatles didn't.

What happened after Brian died? Dick James Music Company—a fuckin' multi-million music-industry company. Northern Songs not owned by us. And NEMS not owned by us. And that was all Brian and his advisors setting it up. What did we end up with? Maybe Paul and I had a hundred thousand or over in the bank, and George and Ringo had about twenty or thirty, something like that.

I mean, I liked Brian, and I had a very close relationship with him for years, like I have with Allen, because I'm not going to have some stranger running the scene, that's all. I also like to be friends with whoever's going to run it . . . I like to work with friends. I was the closest to Brian, as close as you can get to somebody who lives a sort of fag life and you don't know what they're doing on the side. But in the group I was closest to him, and I did like him. He had great qualities and he was good fun. He had a flair. He was a theatrical man rather than a businessman, so in that way I liked him.

But on the business end, he ripped us off on the Seltaeb thing. [Seltaeb, Beatles spelled backward, was the licensee for Beatle products.]

Int.: What makes you say that?

John: It's all coming out in an interview Allen's done for *Playboy*, so maybe you can find it in that. But Brian had made some deal somewhere, and I know we were ripped off by Brian, and the myth is that he was the great, good guy. It's the same as the myth about Paul. Wonderful Paul, and crazy John. And I was always telling Allen, "For Christ's sake, we've got this stuff on Brian. Put it out." I don't care whether

Queenie [Epstein's mother] gets hurt or not. I blame Queenie for what Brian was. Brian was a fag, and in tortured pain, and killed himself. I know she's in pain, and I'm sorry for her, but she ought to know he's a fag and so forth.

Int.: From what I recall about the Seltaeb deal, Brian wasn't careful enough, and he may have given out too many licenses.

John: No, no. Brian did a few things that show he cooked us. We never got anything out of it, and Brian did. But obviously, some things are definite. Just the fact that NEMS was a bigger company than the Beatles. We have no company. There's Northern Songs, NEMS, and Dick James. What did we have? A couple of quid in the bank. That's where Brian fucked up. He's the one who would say, "Sign for another ten years." And who got the benefit? Not us. We're the ones who were tied by the balls.

So that's what I think of him.

Int.: You were saying a few moments ago that Brian was a theatrical man.

John: Well, when he got Cilla Black, his great delight was to dress her and present her. I'm a bit like that, you know, I like to dress Yoko and present her. It's just enjoyment. I think Brian wanted to be a dress designer originally, but his parents stopped it. He would have been a great dress designer, because that's what he was made for.

So with Cilla he was like that, and with us he was a bit like that. He literally fuckin' cleaned us up. And there were great fights between him and me, over years and years, over me not wanting to dress up, and he and Paul wanting me to dress up. In fact, he and Paul had some kind of collusion to keep me straight.

Int.: Paul was eager to dress up?

John: Yeah. But I kept spoiling the image. Like the time I beat up Bob Wooller [a Cavern disc jockey] at Paul's twenty-first. The first national press we got was the back page of the *Daily Mirror* with me beating up Bob Wooller at Paul's twenty-first. That was the first Lennon-hits-out story.

Int.: Your Errol Flynn act again?

John: Yeah. So that was the first national stuff we got. And that was terrible. And I was so bad the next day. We had a BBC appointment, and they all went down in the train, and I wouldn't come. And Brian came to my house and was pleading with me to go down there. And I was saying, "I'm not

... fucking hell," I was so afraid of the outcome, of nearly killing Wooller. Because I nearly killed him. He'd insinuated that me and Brian had had an affair in Spain. I was out of me mind with drink. You know, when you get down to the point where you want to drink out of all the empty glasses, that drunk. And he was saying, "Come on, John, tell me"—something like that—"tell me about you and Brian, we all know." And obviously I must have been frightened of the fag in me to get so angry. You know, when you're twenty-one, you want to be a man, and all that. If somebody said it now, I wouldn't give a shit. So I was beating the shit out of him, and hitting him with a big stick, too, and it was the first time I thought, "I can kill this guy." I just saw it, like on a screen—that if I hit him once more, that was going to be it. And that's when I gave up violence, because all me life I'd been like that, you know. And that's when I really got shocked. And from then on, I've never ... apart from occasionally hitting my dear wife [faint chuckles], in the early days when I was a bit crazy ...

So I can't say I'm nonviolent, because I'll go crazy sometimes. But that was the first fright I had. So I stopped doing that. Anyway, that's nothing to do with it, I tend to dribble on, because you've put me on the path.

Int.: So what did you think of Brian's ability to get a show together?

John: Well, we had complete faith in him, when he was running us. I mean, if you're asking me in retrospect, and I say he made those mistakes, you'd say, well, what a silly businessman. But to us he was the expert. I mean, originally he had a shop. Anybody's who got a shop must be all right. And a car, and a big house ... I mean, fuckin' hell, you don't care if it's all his dad or not. That means "they're it," aren't they? So we thought he was "it." And he got us to EMI. It was his walking round . . . if he hadn't gone round London, on foot, with the tapes under his arm, and gone from place to place, and place to place, and finally to George Martin, we would never have made it. Because we didn't have the push to do it on our own.

Paul was more aggressive in that way. Let's think up publicity stunts, or jump in the Mersey, or something like that in those kind of terms, to make it. So he and Paul got along well in that respect, you know. But he and Paul didn't get along a lot, too, because anybody's who's got anything to say, Paul hates. Like Stuart Sutcliffe, Paul hated him. And they ended up fighting on stage. Paul was saying something about Stu's girl, and he was jealous because she was a great girl, and Stu hit him on stage. And Stu wasn't a violent guy at all. So it was a bit like that between the two of them [McCartney and Epstein] as well.

So Brian seemed a great manager. He got us on EMI. He used to come back from London, and he couldn't face us because he'd been down about twenty times, and he'd come back to say, "Well, I'm afraid they didn't accept it again." And by then we were a bit close to him, and he'd be really hurt. He'd be terrified to tell us that we had not made it again. He did all that. He went around, smarming and charming everybody, the newspaper people—and they all thought highly of him. He's got a good reputation mainly.

He had hellish tempers and fits and lockouts and he'd vanish for days—not like Allen, who just thinks other things are more important than you or me. But with Brian, he would just flip out. He'd come to a crisis now and then, and the whole business would fuckin' stop because he'd been on sleeping pills for days on end, and wouldn't wake up for days. Or beaten up by some docker on the Old Kent Road. So suddenly the whole business would stop and Brian would be missing [laughs].

We weren't too aware of it. It was later on we started finding out about those things. But he sold us, he presented us. He did all that for us. So in a way we would never have made it without him, and vice versa. Like, what I think about the Beatles is, even if it had been Paul and John and two other people, we'd never have been the Beatles. It had to take that combination of Paul, John, George, and Ringo to make the Beatles. There's no such thing as, "Well, John and Paul wrote all the songs, so therefore they contributed more," because if it hadn't been us, we would have got songs from somewhere else maybe, or whatever. And so Brian contributed as much as us in the early days, although we were the talent and he was the hustler.

And we had plenty of ideas. All the early clothes things really came through me from art school. Because the people at art school were wearing hair longer anyway . . .

Yoko: And black . . .

John: . . . and black corduroy, and all that kind of early gear that we would wear, was direct from my art school. So we looked arty, compared with other groups, who looked like clerks or dockers. Whereas we looked like students, which we weren't, but we were still at school. So we had a bit of a classy touch straightaway, which was different, and with a classy, well-spoken manager, and all that. It was a cinch really. But there was a lot of heavy grind for Brian in the early days, and he was good at handling the tours, I think. Once we went to Italy and never got paid, and in Manila he nearly got us killed.

Int.: That was the palace invitation.

John: Yeah, that was Brian's cock-up. Because he'd had the invitation given to him, and declined it, and never told us. And the next day they wouldn't accept that we'd declined it and were hustling and pushing us around at the airport, and wouldn't help us with our bags. It was terrifying. Do you know that story?

Int.: Yes.

John: That was terrifying. That was awful.

Int.: So in the later years did Brian's protective-ness of you all ever become overbearing?

John: No, no. Because he wasn't strong enough to overbear us, we were too strong. You see, people have two images. Like George Martin did everything and the Beatles did nothing. Or the Beatles did everything and

George Martin was invisible. Or Brian Epstein did everything. It was never like that. It was a combination. Brian could never make us do what we *really, really* didn't want to do. He came to us in Paris once and said he'd had enough, and he wanted to sell us to Delfont or Grade, I've forgotten which one. And we all told him—I told him personally—that we would stop. We all said it: "Whatever you do, if you do that, we stop now. We don't play anymore, and we disband. We're not going to let anybody else have us, especially them." Because, after all, we knew already who they were ... they'd been the enemy from the start. It was people like them who Brian had come up against who said, "Go back to the provinces, sonny," and all that shit that he'd been given from all those big-time Londoners who all come from Poland.

Int.: Grade or Delfont?

John: I don't know which one it was, but that *gang* of people who own Britain, you know ... the whole pile. They own England ... the brothers, the sisters, all of them. So that was the enemy, and you didn't want to get caught in with those people. And Brian was going to "cave in" and give us to these fucking people, and he would just look after the light side of life, and those monsters would be running us, and making us do what Richenburg [the head of a company that bought NEMS] said: "Give us what the public wants," and all that. They don't understand, those Richenburgs and Grades. They couldn't handle people like us. They're used to them donkeys that they used to have after the war, Tommy Hanley and all them people, and the poor, old "Crazy Gang," who, like Derek used to say, look like they'd been injected with silicone to be brought onstage at eighty still [laughs].

So whenever Brian tried to make us do something, we didn't care whether it was legal or not. It's the same now. If anything happened, I wouldn't give a shit whether it was legal or not. I'd fuck off, and let them catch me. Let them come and chase me to fucking Japan or Africa, and get me to fucking work if I don't want to. Piss on 'em. So no contract would hold us. So Brian was never overbearing, and if Brian and Paul and everybody said, "Well, look, why don't we just trim our hair a bit and look like this," you're going to say all right in the end, you know, or fuck it. I'll just loosen me collar, or something, you know. So it never got too bad like that. And he wasn't overbearing, no.

Int.: As you watched Brian deteriorate . . .

John: Well, I didn't watch him deteriorate. There was a period of about two years before he died when we didn't hardly see anything of him. After we stopped touring, he had nothing to do really. The money just came in from records. Billy Jay and all them were sort of sinking fast, and all his other protégés, his bullfighters and all those people, were sort of vanishing. And he had nothing to do with us. So really, we grew apart. And like, whenever somebody dies, you think, "If only I'd spoken a bit more to him, he might have been a bit happier." I felt guilty because I was closer to him earlier, and then for two years I was on me own, I was having me own problems, internal, for those two years. And we didn't see him hardly at all, and I had no idea of the kind of life he was living, or anything. And it was always very embarrassing, "Shall we have dinner together?" So we didn't see him, and then he died.

And with the four of us and him, it was heavy people. And there would be an atmosphere, and we'd gradually break it down, and turn him on to acid and all that jazz. Or try and straighten him out—which was what we were trying to do. But he didn't. He died instead.

Int.: So then came Apple. Wasn't there about eight hundred thousand to capitalize Apple?

John: Yeah, by the Beatles selling themselves to Apple. It was the same deal as Northern Songs. See, although Apple turned into the Beatles' baby, Apple was conceived by the Epsteins and NEMS before we took over, before we said: "It's going to be like this." They had it lined up so we would do the same as Northern Songs, sell ourselves to ourselves.

And what happened with Northern Songs was we ended up selling Lenmac, or one of them, forever. That's what fucking Epstein did to us. We lost all our copyrights and Lew Grade's got 'em. And the same idea was behind the Apple thing. They were going to set it up, sell eighty percent to the public, and we were going to be twenty percent minority shareholders, with five percent each, and God knows who else running it. And that was the idea for Apple, but I dunno, it got screwed up somehow.

Int.: Wasn't Apple Paul's idea, basically?

John: No, no.

Int.: Not even the development of it?

John: Into what?

Int.: A sort of foundation.

John: Oh, no. No. That was us all talking, just about what we wanted to do. See, initially Clive Epstein [Brian's brother] came up to us and said, "You've got so much money and we're thinking of investing it into retail shops for you." You can just imagine the Beatles with a string of retail fuckin' shoe shops—that was the way they thought. They were still on Queens Drive in Liverpool, mentally. Clive Epstein still is, all he wants to do is get back in the hills. So we said, "We don't want to be. Imagine us owning fucking retail shops." So we said, "We don't want to be in that. At least if we're going to open a shop, let's open something that we'd want, that we'd like to buy." We were thinking, "Let's be the Woolworth of something." Or how great it was to go into Marks and Spencer and get a decent sweater when you were about eighteen. Cheap, but good quality. We wanted Apple to be that. So we were just tripping off, having a joint and saying, "Well, we could have films, and we could help young artists, so they wouldn't have to have the trouble we had with all that tramping round, being undiscovered. So we just built it up. This is what we're going to do. We could have a foundation, and all that, which could have been feasible.

Int.: And you ended up with a clothes shop on Baker Street.

John: We ended up with a clothes shop. I don't know how. This group of people, The Fool, suddenly turned up. I don't know where they came from. I think they came through Paul or George. And then I brought in "Magic Alex" [the inventor], and it just went from bad to worse.

Int.: How soon did you realize that it wasn't going to turn out the way you wanted?

John: I don't know. I don't remember. It was going on and on. And then I got a letter saying what was going on at Apple, and that's that bit.

Int.: Were you disappointed with the whole Apple thing, about not being able to get it together financially?

John: No, it wasn't that. Because originally we didn't want an Apple. Clive Epstein said, like they did every few years, if you don't do this it will go in taxes. They said, "It's going to go in taxes, so we have to do this new scheme." So we really didn't want an Apple, or to go into fucking business, but the thing was, if we have to go in, let's go into something we like. And then Clive Epstein didn't like any of our ideas. We said, "Well, let's sell groovy clothes or something." Or Paul came up with a nice idea, which was, let's sell everything white. You can never get anything white, like cups and all that. Which is right. I've been looking for a decent set of white cups for five years. I don't know where the name Apple came from, Paul or Mal, I'm not sure. And it just developed from that.

I was just disappointed that all this money went to cock, and that it was embarrassing in public to be stuck with a big monster. And of course, like everything we go into, we're as enthusiastic as shit, you know. We really thought there would be millions, and we'd be able to help a lot of people with it. Well, we did. But the wrong ones.

Int.: Do you remember when you and Paul came to announce the whole thing on the *Tonight* show?

John: Yes, yes. Oh, it was terrible. There was a baseball player hosting the show, and they didn't tell us.

Int.: Joe Garagiola.

John: Yeah, and he was asking, "Which one's Ringo?" and all that shit. You'd expect to go on the Johnny Carson show . . . and then you get there, and there's this sort of football player, who doesn't know anything about you, and Tallulah Bankhead, pissed out of her head, saying how beautiful we were. It was the most embarrassing thing I've ever been on.

Int.: The only thing that came across was that you had lots of money to give away.

Yoko: That's bad.

John: Anyway, Yoko came up with the idea of giving all the Apple stuff away. And we did. That was the best thing that ever happened to Apple. It was a big event, and all the kids came and just took everything that was in the shop. That was the best thing about the whole shop, when we gave it all away. But the night before we all went in and took what we wanted ... it wasn't much ... T-shirts ...

Yoko: It was great.

John: It was great, it was like robbing. We took everything we wanted home. And the next day we were watching, and there were thousands of kids all going in and getting their freebees. It was just great. Of course, Derek and the others hated it, but it so happened that I was running the office at that time, so we were in control. Paul had called me up one day, and said, "I'm going away. You take over."

Int.: It was as simple as that.

John: Yeah, it was as stupid as that.

Int.: During that time, after Brian died . . .

John: We were with Maharishi . . .

Int.: Right, and then you came back, and there was the making of *Magical Mystery Tour*. Did Paul ever play the role of businessman, as if he were going to take charge of everything?

John: Well, *Magical Mystery Tour* was another film that none of us really wanted to make, except for Paul. We didn't know anything about it, till we were halfway through. It was literally like, Paul would come into this circle and say, "This is *Magical Mystery Tour*. Would you write that bit? And I was choked that he'd arranged it all with Mal Evans anyway, for a kickoff, and had all this idea going. And he comes in and says, "We're all going to do this."

I was still under a false impression. I still felt every now and then that Brian would come in and say, "It's time to record," or "Time to do this." And Paul started doing that. "Now we're going to make a movie. Now we're going to make a record." And he assumed that if he didn't call us, nobody would ever make a record. Well, it's since shown that we managed quite well to make records on time. I don't have any schedule. I just think, "Now I'll make it." But in those days Paul would say, well, now he felt like it. And suddenly I'd have to whip out twenty songs. He'd come in with about twenty good songs and say, "We're recording." And I had to suddenly write a fucking stack of songs. Like, *Pepper* was like that. And *Magical Mystery Tour* was another. So I hastily did my bits for it, and we went out on the road, and Paul did his thing that he did for his album, the big-timer auditioning directors. And what fucking directors. We didn't get directors, we got cameramen who walked in. And what we say to them is: "Are you a director?" And they say, "Yes." And we say, "Are you any good?" and he says, "Yes." And we say, "Well, you're on." And that's the big business scene, you know.

So that's how it was. It was just fucking rubbish and cockeyed. I think I brought in Dennis O'Dell, because I'd seen him work on *How I Won the War*, and he was pretty good on that because he'd got everything free, the army things.

Int.: But before *Mystery Tour* there was *Pepper*. We could talk a lot about that, but let me ask you this: did Paul time his famous LSD announcement to coincide with the release of *Pepper*? I mean, when he first took it, wasn't *Pepper* under way.

John: No, we'd had acid on *Revolver*.

Int.: Paul had?

John: Yes, yes. Everybody's under this illusion. Even George Martin saying, "*Pepper* was their acid album." But we'd had acid including Paul, by the time *Revolver* was finished.

Int.: So why did he make that big announcement?

John: Because the press had cornered him. I don't know how they found out that he was taking it, but the press suddenly got on to it and went to his house. But that was a year after we'd all taken it. So *Rubber Soul* was the pot album, and *Revolver* was acid. I mean, we weren't all stoned making *Rubber Soul* because in those days we couldn't work on pot. We never recorded under acid, or anything like that. It's like saying, "Did Dylan Thomas write *Under Milk Wood* on beer?" What the fuck does that have to do with it? The beer is to prevent the rest of the world from crowding in on you. The drugs are to prevent the rest of the world from crowding in on you. They don't make you write any better. I never wrote any better stuff because I was on acid, or not on acid, you know.

Int.: So regardless of what was true about *when* you were taking drugs, when *Pepper* came out, and after Paul made his announcement, everybody discovered what was going on. It didn't matter really that *Rubber Soul* was pot or that *Revolver* was acid, what mattered was that kids, especially in the U.S., perceived *Pepper* as an acid trip in itself.

John: Well, it was the same with everything, like the Beatle haircuts and the Beatle round-neck jackets and the Beatle boots. *Pepper* was just an evolvement of the Beatle boots, and all that. It was just another psychedelic image, you know. Beatle haircuts and boots were just as big as flowered pants in their time. The initial round-neck jackets were Cardin, and were available in shops anyway, and so were the army coats that we wore.

Int.: So what did you think about all those kids who felt that in order to get into wearing flowered pants, they had to take acid?

John: Well, that was never said. Nobody ever said anything like that.

Int.: Would you have preferred it if *Pepper* had been seen as simply a pure work of art?

John: Well, I never felt that when *Pepper* came out, Haight-Ashbury was a direct result. It always seemed to me that they were sort of happening all at once. It was like the Cardin jackets. We bought them from a store. The army jackets—kids were already wearing army jackets on the King's Road, all we did was make them famous. The haircuts—many art students I'd seen for ten years before had had the haircut. We made them famous, that's all.

Yoko: And acceptable. And also, the acid scene was going on a long time before that in America.

John: Right. Leary was the one who was going round saying, "Take it, take it, take it." And we followed his instructions, in *The Book of the Dead*, his how-to-take-a-trip book. And I did it just like he said in the book, and then I wrote "Tomorrow Never Knows," which is on *Revolver*, and which is almost the first acid song—"lay down all thought, surrender to the void," and all that shit which Leary had pinched from *The Book of the Dead*.

I read that George Martin was saying that John was into *The Book of the Dead*. I'd never seen it in me life. I just saw Leary's psychedelic handout—it was very nice in them days.

Int.: But if you consider the important social forces in the sixties, the name of the group has to come up?

John: Right.

Int.: Did you ever think much about the effect you had on kids?

John: What, you mean turning them on to acid?

Int.: Among other things.

John: I don't ever feel responsible for turning them on to acid. Because I don't think we did anything to kids, anything somebody does they do to themselves. It's like *Two Virgins*. We didn't create nudity, we just put it out. Somebody else had been nude before. Avant-garde people had done nudity, and jazz drummers had been into heroin ... we knew people who were on "H" in Liverpool before we really knew anything about it, or drugs, or things like that. We just heard about all those famous drummers in England, the jazz drummers, and we were just being traditional musicians taking drugs, as far as we were concerned. Every musician we met, from the jazz or the rock world, was taking some kind of drug. And acid was just another drug.

Yoko: [To John] But you had some kind of aura or sparkle, you know. I mean, Richard Alpert and Timothy Leary both were into acid, but Timothy Leary supposedly is the cult hero, and Alpert isn't. There's that bit about it, definitely. You had the power to influence.

John: Did Paul's statement on acid come out after *Sergeant Pepper*?

Int.: April 1967.

John: Was that after *Sergeant Pepper* or before it?

Int.: Just as it was released.

John: I see. He always times his big announcements right on the letter, doesn't he? Like leaving the Beatles. Maybe it's instinctive. It probably is. He's got a timing for it. But anyway, "Lucy in the Sky with Diamonds" is not about LSD, and "Henry the Horse" is not about "horse" on *Sergeant Pepper*, because I'd never even seen it when we made *Sergeant Pepper*. But those kind of stories evolved from it— listening to it backward and it says "Paul is dead"—all that shit is just gobbledygook.

Int.: So it's what the kids believed. Even so, with drugs, a great many kids who might never have followed Timothy Leary did follow the Beatles.

John: Yeah [laughs]. Well, I blame it on Dylan. He turned us on to pot in the St. Regis Hotel in 1964. Incidentally, Dylan turned blacks on to pretty hair, and nobody ever states that. Dylan was the first guy with a natural. Jimi Hendrix copied Dylan, and the blacks copied Jimi Hendrix. So I hope our Black Panther friends will remember that when they come for us.

Yoko: But many things happened this way, and I think it's so interesting as history, that none of them really were aware of what was happening . . .

John: We weren't. We weren't aware of what was happening.

Yoko: There was no sense of "Let's turn them on to acid." It wasn't like that . . . But I think the most important thing the Beatles did was to show the kids that you don't have to be born an aristocrat, or you don't have to be born an intellectual to make it . . . you can make it young . . . you can make it working class.

John: But many young people had made it before us, and besides, Elvis had done that.

Yoko: I know, but they didn't start to realize it as a big hope thing ... because Elvis was never an—

John: Yes he was, he was bigger ... well, he wasn't bigger than us, but he was "the thing," you know. He had just the same impact. He just wasn't articulate, that's all.

Int.: What did you think of Elvis when you met him?

John: Oh, I don't know. It was just nice meeting Elvis. He was just Elvis, you know. He played a few songs, and we were all playing guitars. It was great. We never talked about anything. We just played music.

Yoko: But to get back to what we were saying ... after the Beatles so many people emerged from the working class. Like, in the old days, you had to talk snob English. Now, you can't even get a job modeling or something unless you talk working class.

John: Yeah, but like I said, that all really began with *Look Back In Anger*. We came through the *Look Back In Anger*, *Goon Show* thing, which was breaking through all those things ...

Yoko: Yeah, but you assimilated it and synthe-
sized it.

John: I know, but we were the sons of the
Goon Show. We were of age. We were just
the extension of that rebellion, in a way.

Int.: When you think about how the Beatles
evolved, through Liverpool, Hamburg, all
that playing together, what do you think
of the way so-called groups get packaged
and merchandized these days?

John: You mean the way they just put one
together?

Int.: Yes.

John: Well, they used to do that in the past.
This has been going on since time began.
They used to have fifty Drifters. When the
Drifters were a big thing, they used to have
half a dozen of them performing all over
the place. They manufactured singers in
the twenties too. Like in the film *Citizen
Kane*, when he manufactured the opera
singer. Kings would make famous opera
singers out of their mistresses. That's always been going on. It's only the same
shit.

Int.: How do you think the recording "industry"
affects the music today, the fact that it's all
raw dollars?

John: But it always was, though. There's nothing different. I don't know why anybody thinks it's any different than it ever was. It just might be more money and more people, but there's more money, there's more people, there's more everything. So relatively, it's no different as far as I can see. I'm sure that Shakespeare was ripped off, and that there were many little Shakespeares put together when he was popular.

Int.: You don't think something that's as obviously bad as Grand Funk Railroad has an effect on the overall quality of the music?

John: I don't think it does. It balances out, it equals out. More people can assimilate more shit, but the shit is relatively the same as it ever was. But if something good comes out, it can get to a larger audience. So I think it's yin-yang. It will balance out that way.

Int.: Before we turned the tape on, you were saying something about your plans as filmmakers. What was that?

John: Oh, right. I'd like to go to Russia. A friend of ours just came back and said we'd be most welcome there. They could get us an invite, and maybe we could go quietly as filmmakers. But they'd probably want us to go as rock.

Int.: But not Beatle rock?

John: No, I'm not resurrecting that.

Int.: So to come back to what we were talking of earlier ... having written so much with Paul, do you think it's possible for there to be some type of settlement, or rapprochement, outside of business? And if it's feasible, would you be prepared to take some kind of initiative in that?

John: Well, there's no way for it to be settled "outside business," because it all gets down to who owns a bit of what. And it has to be that way. It's a house we own together and there's no way of settling it, unless we all decide to live in it. It has to be sold.

Int.: So, have you missed writing songs with Paul?

John: No, I haven't. I wrote alone in the early days. We used to write separately. He was writing songs before I even started writing songs. I think he was, anyway. And we'd written separately for years. I mean, in *Help*, I wrote "Help." I wrote "A Hard Day's Night." He wrote "Yesterday." They'd been separate for years.

In the early days we only ever wrote together for fun, and later on for convenience, to get so many numbers out for an album. But our best songs were always written alone. And things like "A Day in the Life" was just my song and his song stuck together. So the collaboration myth about ... I mean, we used to sit down and finish each other's songs off. You know, you could have three quarters of a song finished and we'd just sit together, bring our ten songs each, and just finish off the tail ends, and put middle eights in ones you couldn't be bothered fixing because it wasn't all that good anyway.

We usually got together on songs that were less interesting. Now and then we'd write together from scratch. Well, quite often in fact ... things like "I Wanna Hold Your Hand," things like that were done like that. But we'd been working apart ever since we were working together. So it was no great news, it was only news to the public, that a lot of them Lennon-McCartney songs weren't Lennon-McCartney. But that was something we'd agreed on years ago.

Int.: Do you think it was a mistake in retrospect to have done it that way, Lennon McCartney?

John: No, I don't, because it worked very well when it was useful. It's just no longer useful.

Then it was useful so it was quite good fun. I've nothing against it.

Int.: So if you got—I don't even know what the right phrase is—"back together now?" What would the nature of it be?

John: Well, it's like saying, if you were back in your mother's womb. I don't fucking know. It's a mad question. What can I answer? It will never happen, so there's no use contemplating it.

Yoko: They've outgrown ...

John: Even if we were ... even if I'm friends with Paul again, I'd never write with him again. There's no point, you know. I might write with Yoko because she's in the same room as me.

Yoko: And we're living together ...

John: And we're living together. So it's natural. I was living with Paul then, so I wrote with him. It's whoever you're living with. He writes with Linda, he's living with her, you know. So it's just natural.

ABOUT THE AUTHORS

PETER MCCABE has worked as a writer and editor for a number of magazines, including *Rolling Stone*, *Penthouse*, and *Harper's*. He is now Senior Editor at *Manhattan inc*. He lives in New York City.

ROBERT SCHONFELD, a recent graduate of NYU School of Business at the time this interview was done, is now Senior Vice President of Hirschl & Adler Galleries.